BOOK OF Hope

Greetings, thank you for hearing the words from this book. It is the story of the Creator's greatest gift, the gift of His Son Jesus of the Tribe of Judah. The Native Book of Hope will help you find the trail of peace, purpose, and power for your life.

The Native American Fellowship

greetings!

BOOK OF *hope*

Long ago, the Creator came to earth to take on the form of a Man, so Jesus was born into the tribe of Judah, a brown-skinned and dark-haired people.

He had just 12 followers at the beginning, but now people from every tribe, clan, nation and language are following the trail of **hope**.

The *Native Book of Hope* shows us why Jesus was willing to give the greatest gift ever given to bring all Native people back to the Creator; how the power of Jesus is able to overcome evil spirits, fear, diseases and even death; and how you can find peace, purpose, and power for your life by following the trail of **hope**.

This book tells the story of the Creator's love for all people. On pages 4-21, you can read the stories of Native people whose lives have changed as a result of meeting the Creator. The story of the Creator begins on page 33. The story is divided into sections such as 1.1 or 2.10 for reference purposes.

Read it and find His love for you.

contents

Stories of Hope*......................................page 4
    Pain/Hope ....page 4   4.30
    Addiction/Victory...................................page 6   3.53
    Anger/Comfort.......................................page 8   3.7
    Abandoned/Secure ....page 11   5.31
    Rejected/Accepted ....page 12   4.75
    Damaged/Restored ....page 15   4.76
    Empty/Full ....page 16   4.38
    Unloved/Wanted ....page 19   2.13
    Broken/Healed ....page 20   4.57
    Lost/Found ....page 21   5.32

Trail of Hope ....page 22

Thank you...page 32

Book of Hope ....page 33-189

Ancestry of Jesus ....page 190

Timeline...page 192

Dictionary..page 193

Index..page 199

What is the Book of Hope? ....page 208

*The stories of Hope are true, but the names have been changed and are not referenced to any person.

pain

At thirteen I started to drink, hang around the bars, and go out with anyone that showed an interest in me, and having a son at the age of sixteen didn't change my lifestyle at all. I gave the responsibility of motherhood over to my mother and sisters. A year later I was pregnant again. I felt no obligation whatsoever toward these two innocent children.

I took acid and smoked pot along with the rest of the crowd, just so I could be involved in their "fun." One time I tried heroin to make me feel "in," but, unfortunately, I found that I craved it again after only one try. Using heroin made me feel, for the first time in my life, that I was somebody. I thought I was no longer an outsider, a loner, caught in a life of confusion. However, unanswered questions filled my mind during both the good and the bad highs. "Is this all there is to living? Will I be a prisoner until I die? What then?"

Bondage

During this time I was blessed with another son. I lied to myself, thinking I could change, but I continued to submit to my drug addiction. Though I tried not to use heroin so much, that craving was still there; without it, my emotions surfaced. The temper I didn't know I had exploded more often. Depression became my number one buddy, but somehow I made it through that pregnancy, too.

Then it was back to the old crowd. I got the heroin for free, but I paid for it during withdrawal. It seemed I wasn't going to survive the torture. I craved that brown liquid of instant magic. I could even feel the needle in my vein and imagine the effects of it just by closing my eyes and remembering.

There was no way to relieve the pain because I had no money to continue to satisfy my addiction. At this time I felt as if I had no reason to live. Nobody mattered at all. I wanted to hurt people any way I could, and I did.

I went back to drinking anything that would help me forget the mess I had made of my life. I couldn't get away from alcohol no matter how

hard I tried. I desperately wanted to believe that someday I'd be set free. Yet, I didn't think I would ever know true peace.

One Last Look

I was about to slip deeper into my world of nothingness, but I decided to look for love and acceptance one more time. I searched the faces of people who once told me they loved me. There was something different about my three aunts who attended an Assemblies of God church.

They spoke the same words of love for me with outstretched arms and warm embraces. Their love actually caught me off guard. Deep inside I knew there might still be hope for me.

I had been invited to church many times, but I always had an excuse for not going. This time I went, even though I wasn't sure why. Now I know it was the Holy Spirit drawing me to that church.

In January, I found what I had longed for all those lifeless, miserable years. That night I accepted Jesus Christ as my personal Savior. I experienced a miraculous change in my life. I received the love, joy, and peace that I had previously been searching for. Yes, I've had struggles since that night, and I have stumbled. But Jesus is there to pick me up and give me the power to overcome. He said He will never leave me or forsake me.

Another wonderful thing happened that I never dreamed would come true: the Lord gave me a husband.

Your Second Chance

If you are going through the same pattern of life that I lived, believe me; what you are searching for can only be found in Jesus Christ. It is not too late for you. I'm a living testimony of His miracle-working power. He is the God who gives a second chance at life.

Chris Manuel
Tohono O'Odam

See Section 4.30 for the story of another person who got a second chance.

addiction

"What if we have a car wreck today and I die? Where am I going to go?" That thought ran through my mind as we headed out of town. I was too young to die. I had barely turned eighteen. The first eighteen years didn't seem all that bad, even though it was hard growing up in an alcoholic family. But to me it was natural, since I had never known anything else.

I sat there thinking about the days when I panhandled and hustled on the streets with my stepfather. I began drinking when I was around ten years old. I used to sneak beer from parties and drink by myself. Before long I started drinking wine and whiskey. My drug addiction followed.

In the sixth grade, I started fooling around with marijuana, speed, and LSD. Drugs seemed to get a grip on me even quicker than alcohol. I quit school in the seventh grade and gave all my time to satisfying my habit.

One day while I was still on the reservation, my friends and I got high and partied nonstop. We drove around that day and decided to park out of town where we wouldn't be as likely to get stopped by the police. We finally came to a place where we felt it was safe to stop. As my brother Johnny was sitting next to me, he began to roll a joint.

Hopeful Future

While that was happening, these questions echoed over and over in my mind. "What if we have a car wreck today and I die? Where am I going to go?" I knew exactly where I was going—straight to hell.

After Johnny finished rolling the joint, he handed it to me and said, "Here you go."

With death already on my mind, those rods felt like somebody was taking a gun, putting it to my head, and saying, "Here you go; you are going to die today." My heart started pounding, and my palms got sweaty.

I got out of the car and walked behind it. Then I knelt down and said, "Lord, if there is any way you can change my life, change it. If there is any way you can make me a testimony to my friends and family, do it. I don't want to go to hell, and I don't want them to go there either."

As I was kneeling there praying, I heard my friends talking. One of them asked, "What's he doing back there?" Another answered, "It looks like he's praying!"

The car door opened, and one of my friends walked around to the back of the car. Part of me felt like getting up and saying that I had stomach cramps and that everything was alright, but the other part of me said, "If you get up, it's just like telling God that you didn't mean a word of what you just said."

As my friend stood there looking at me, I continued to pray asking God's forgiveness and mercy upon my life. After a while my friend got back into the car. The peace of God flooded my soul. I knew, as I got up from my knees, God had forgiven me and given me a new life in Him. God no longer looked down from heaven with a frown on His face. Now there was a twinkle in His eye.

Within one month of my roadside conversion, I went to Bible college, even though I didn't have a high school diploma or a G.E.D. There I learned how to pray, study the Bible, and really serve God. I graduated with a Bachelor of Arts Degree in Ministerial Studies. I currently serve as a pastor. My wife and I have three children.

God changed my life. He can change your life too.

Danny Brant
Mohawk

See Section 3.53 for the story of another man who was set free.

ange

I grew up on the Fort Peck Reservation in Montana. Both of my parents were alcoholics. They separated when I was about sixteen, and that caused me the typical trauma that comes from a broken home.

I spent six years in a reformatory, except for a few times when they released me because of my problems with alcohol and fighting. Those times were opportunities to "catch up" with the crowd back home.

When I was in school, I did well and even had an "A" average during my sophomore year. I finished my junior year at eighteen and was allowed to go home for a short vacation. I never went back. I spent the next year working my way through Idaho, California, and Arizona. Though I was a good worker, I usually spent the weekends drinking.

When I returned to the reservation in the spring, there was no incentive to do anything but follow the crowd. Within a few weeks, I was in serious trouble (the charge—assault with a deadly weapon, the sentence—four to six years in the federal prison in Lompoc, California).

When I made parole, I swore I would not be back in prison. I went home, and within three weeks, I was with "my crowd" when they stole some liquor. I ended up back in Lompoc.

It felt like an eternity before they released me again. Now twenty-two years old, I had spent nearly ten years of my life incarcerated in institutions, jails, and prison. It seemed like there was no way for me because I was always getting drunk and ending up in trouble. Alcohol and my anger did not mix.

I continued my run-ins with the law; once I got kicked off the reservation for a year, except for emergencies. During that time my father died from a heart condition, my mother died from alcoholism, and my brother was killed in a bar.

The things that happened to me in all those years of trouble filled me with anger, hatred toward authority, and bitterness toward society. I resented wasting so many years locked up, and I blamed others for my loss.

When I quit my job and moved back to the rez, I got involved with drugs. One day the police raided my house looking for drugs. They didn't find any, but the raid deepened my anger, so I threatened the officer who initiated the search. The next morning I pulled alongside his police car and pointed a rifle at him and another officer. As they pulled away, I shot over their car.

While looking down the double barrels of that gun, I heard what I believed was the voice of God say in a quiet but firm tone, "Get out very slowly." A quietness and calm I had never known before swept over me. Slowly, slowly, I got out of my car. I was jailed and charged with "assault with a deadly weapon." At my initial trial, I pled not guilty and was allowed out on bond.

One day I went into the bathroom to take some drugs. As I stood there with the pills in my hand, I decided to "fix" the police for causing me all this trouble. I thought, "I'll make them sorry they ever raided my house. I'll bring all the drugs I can onto this reservation. I'll be the 'number one' man. I'll teach them to mess with me. I'm going all the way."

That very moment God spoke to me again and said, "Johnny, you're wrong." When I heard that voice, I saw my life flash before me. I saw myself as I really was. It hurt to see how I had treated my family, so I cried out, "Lord, forgive me!"

When I called out to God in sorrow for what I had done, I saw prison bars that were like doors. Those doors swung open and away from me with such a force that I almost fell backward. I was free!

I walked out of the bathroom a different man. Many changes took place in my life. First, I started praying about everything, and I couldn't get enough of the Bible. I started going to church.

BOOK OF HOPE 9

anger

I was still facing the "assault with a deadly weapon" charge. But I changed my plea to guilty, so my lawyer dropped my case. I just put myself in the Lord's hands.

The judge for my case was the same one who had once told me, "If you ever come before this court again, I'll throw the book at you." This time, he looked at me and said, "Johnny, you are an intelligent man. I am giving you five years' probation."

Not long after this, our little boy, William, passed away. Before he died, my wife April prayed, "Lord, if you will save my boy, I'll serve you." Then she changed her prayer and said, "No, Lord, no matter what, I'll serve you." That day, God changed our lives. William's death brought April to the Lord and drew us closer together. Since then God has blessed us with four more children.

My wife and I have served the Lord since that time.

When those spiritual prison doors swung open for me, I walked out a new person. You may not be in jail, but if you have never given your life to Christ, you're in a spiritual prison. No matter where you are, call out to Him right now. You don't have to pray a long prayer. Just mean it from your heart like I did when I said, "Lord, forgive me."

That was the shortest prayer I ever prayed, but it made the greatest impact on my life. God heard my cry. He will hear yours. Tell Him you are sorry for the way you have lived. Ask Him to forgive you and change you. He will!

Johnny Fox
Assiniboine Sioux

See Section 3.7 for the story of another person who experienced freedom.

comfort

BOOK OF HOPE

NO abandoned

When I was a child, even into my teens, the idea of a nurturing "home" and "family" didn't exist for me. When I was two, my parents got a divorce. My father's struggle with alcoholism was part of the cause. My first memory was of my dad beating my mom.

I also had an older brother who would come in drunk all the time, and he would also beat my mom. As a single parent, my mother really didn't pay much attention to me or my siblings. I was devastated, since she wasn't emotionally there for us.

I was also sexually abused when I was six years old. Time went on, but I always had this pain in my heart. Where was home, and where was family for me? I felt I had nowhere to go and no one to turn to. During the summer, I had been crying every day, and I didn't know how to deal with the pain.

One day I was crying in my room, as usual. I was going through the options for getting rid of my pain. I thought about turning to drugs or alcohol, but I knew what that choice had done to my dad and brother. None of those things were the answer. I thought about talking to someone, but, since I had been hurt so many times, I trusted no one as a true friend to me.

I felt like my options had run out and that the only way to get rid of my pain was suicide. As I was thinking about this, the Lord's presence filled the room. I sensed God saying to me as a caring father would, "You are everything to me." I felt an overwhelming love, joy, and peace in my heart. At that moment I gave my life to Jesus.

I couldn't believe that the Creator of the universe thought that I meant everything to Him when I knew I was nothing. That summer the Lord started a healing process in me. He is the ultimate Parent, my heavenly Father, and my best Friend.

Linda Redsky
Seminole

See Section 5.31 to learn about the security our Heavenly Father has for those who serve Him.

secure (family)

BOOK OF HOPE

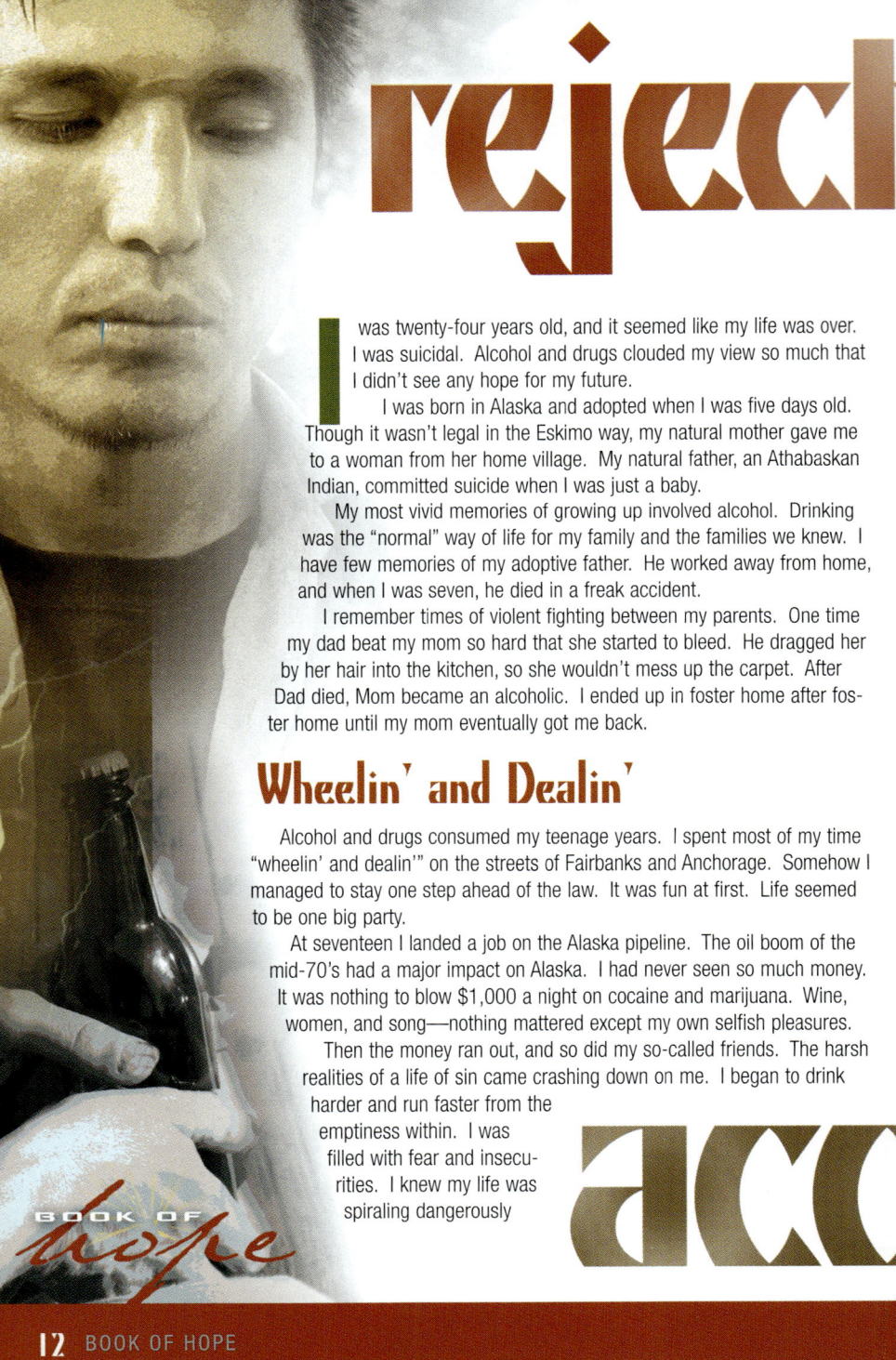

reject

I was twenty-four years old, and it seemed like my life was over. I was suicidal. Alcohol and drugs clouded my view so much that I didn't see any hope for my future.

I was born in Alaska and adopted when I was five days old. Though it wasn't legal in the Eskimo way, my natural mother gave me to a woman from her home village. My natural father, an Athabaskan Indian, committed suicide when I was just a baby.

My most vivid memories of growing up involved alcohol. Drinking was the "normal" way of life for my family and the families we knew. I have few memories of my adoptive father. He worked away from home, and when I was seven, he died in a freak accident.

I remember times of violent fighting between my parents. One time my dad beat my mom so hard that she started to bleed. He dragged her by her hair into the kitchen, so she wouldn't mess up the carpet. After Dad died, Mom became an alcoholic. I ended up in foster home after foster home until my mom eventually got me back.

Wheelin' and Dealin'

Alcohol and drugs consumed my teenage years. I spent most of my time "wheelin' and dealin'" on the streets of Fairbanks and Anchorage. Somehow I managed to stay one step ahead of the law. It was fun at first. Life seemed to be one big party.

At seventeen I landed a job on the Alaska pipeline. The oil boom of the mid-70's had a major impact on Alaska. I had never seen so much money. It was nothing to blow $1,000 a night on cocaine and marijuana. Wine, women, and song—nothing mattered except my own selfish pleasures.

Then the money ran out, and so did my so-called friends. The harsh realities of a life of sin came crashing down on me. I began to drink harder and run faster from the emptiness within. I was filled with fear and insecurities. I knew my life was spiraling dangerously out of control, but I tried to act as if I didn't care. As time went on, I found fewer reasons to live and more reasons to end it all.

The Wreck

Then something happened that God used to change the direction of my life. One summer evening—after I had been drinking and smoking dope since early morning—I went for a ride on my motorcycle. I was on a narrow, two-lane highway south of Anchorage. I came to a straight stretch of the road that goes into a relatively sharp curve. I stomped on the gas and took off like a bullet, trying to slow down near the corner. I misjudged my distance traveling over 80 MPH.

I remember thinking, "I hope there's nobody coming." By that time I was in the oncoming lane. To my horror I saw that I was headed into the front of a big truck. The driver swerved out of the way. I slid past, but the back bumper of the truck caught me just below my left kneecap, and that threw me off my motorcycle. After sliding and rolling down the highway and ending up in a ditch, I was shocked when I looked down at my leg. All I saw was bone and blood from my knee to my ankle.

Running From God

I ended up in the hospital even more angry and bitter. I shared a room with a Christian Eskimo man. At first, I couldn't stand being stuck in the bed next to a "Christian." We had nothing in common. As time passed God used this gentle, loving and very patient man to slowly melt my heart. For the first time since I was a child, I began to wonder if God is real, but I resisted the Spirit's tug on my heart.

I continued to drink and do drugs even more. Now I wasn't just running from the "emptiness within." I was RUNNING FROM GOD! I couldn't get Jesus out of my mind. No matter how much I tried, there He was.

Sick and Tired

Finally, as I sat in a bar one night, I pondered what my life had become. I was surrounded by the same old people, doing the same old thing, going to the same old place—nowhere.

I was sick and tired of being sick and tired.

rejected

Something had to change. I left the bar and started walking. I came to a secluded place, stopped, leaned my head back and yelled, "Jesus, if you're real, then prove yourself to me or just leave me alone!"

Jesus Proves Himself...to Me

When we cry out in the darkest places of our lives, JESUS HEARS US! He cares about sinners at the "end of their rope." Jesus began to "prove" Himself to me. Within a week I met some people I used to party with. They invited me to a little Native church they had started attending. To my own amazement, I went.

I can't really remember the sermon, but I certainly remember the results of that message. God met me that night. I knelt, and with tears flowing, I said, "Jesus, if you can change me and save me, I will serve you the rest of my life."

The Rest of the Story

That happened sixteen years ago. Jesus has kept his side of the "deal," and so have I. I not only met Jesus that wonderful night but also my beautiful wife, Barbara.

After I gave my life to Jesus, my mom ended up in the hospital because of her drinking; she nearly died. But through prayer, she made a miraculous recovery, and I had the wonderful privilege of leading my mom to become a follower of Jesus Christ. She lived the last fifteen years of her life saved and alcohol-free.

Mike Tall
Inupiaq & Athabaskan

See Section 4.75 to see how Jesus treats those who come to Him.

accepted

damaged

I came from a big family. My grandpa was a well-known medicine man and very active in tribal politics. My grandma lived a hard life. She raised me when I was a child because my mom had to leave to find employment. My father abandoned us and never returned. Grandma physically and mentally abused me, making me feel worthless and stupid.

When I was old enough, I was taken to a boarding school. I never felt so alone and abandoned in my life. The staff physically abused us and tried to force us to speak English.

I returned to my people, but it was a bad experience. I no longer spoke Navajo, my appearance had changed, and I behaved differently. I felt rejected and worthless. I started drinking alcohol and doing drugs.

I had nothing to live for, so I tried to commit suicide. By God's grace I met a Christian doctor who said, "You have no right to take God's gift of life and destroy it for your purpose."

My life was like a feather blowing in the wind. I was driving and noticed a family in a rez car. I wondered why they were so happy. I saw a radio bumper sticker on their car. I turned to the station, and someone was preaching the Gospel and giving an invitation to come to know the Creator, Jesus Christ.

I made the decision to ask Jesus to change my life. I can't explain how I felt, except I became a new person. I came home happy, picked up the Bible, and started to read. I also got involved in a local church.

I have a heavenly Father Who loves me unconditionally. I am a part of His royal family. I can tell you now I have peace, love, joy, and a purpose in life.

Nashoni Begay
Navajo

See Section 4.76 to read the story of another person who was restored.

restored

BOOK OF HOPE 15

empty

From my childhood all I remember is sadness. My parents, aunts, and uncles were alcoholics. It seemed as if everyone I knew had a drinking problem. Our house served one main purpose: partying.

I grew up surrounded by booze, drugs, smoking, gambling, fighting, and adultery. I always told myself, "I'm not going to follow my parents' example. I'm going to better myself. My lips will never taste liquor."

In my teen years, my parents decided to get a divorce. They asked us children what we thought about it. We didn't know what to say, so we said nothing. I wish now that I had spoken up and said, "Try to work it out."

After the divorce my uncle moved in. He bought some wine and gave it to me. He said, "Tom, I'm an alcoholic, as are your parents, and you'll be an alcoholic too."

I hid the wine. However, without a father in my life, I felt there was no use in resisting. I started drinking. When booze no longer satisfied, I started smoking marijuana.

From that time I began experimenting with speed, acid, and other drugs. By using speed I discovered I could stay awake and high for several days and nights at a time. I thought that was really cool.

In the midst of all this, I found a girlfriend and dropped out of high school. This girl eventually became my wife. She knew I liked to drink, but she didn't know how bad I really was.

Early in our marriage, a nagging question kept troubling me. "What happens if you die the way you are? Is this life all there is, and when you're dead, there's nothing more?" This thought haunted me, so I continued to drink, smoke, and stay high while trying to silence this voice. It never left me alone. I was searching for something, but I didn't know what.

I scared my two young daughters when I came home drunk one day and fought with my wife and sister-in-law. My wife said, "You're crazy, Tom. I can't take it any more." She left me and filed for a divorce.

Then strange things began to happen. Our divorce lawyer said, "You two are very young. I'm going to put this divorce on hold for a year. Why don't you try and work it out?"

Soon after that my brother-in-law became a born-again Christian, and he urged my wife to pray for me. In a short time, my wife and sister-in-law became born-again Christians.

I called my wife one afternoon to set up a visitation schedule, so I could see my daughters. She told me that she was praying for me and that she believed in God.

I said, "You don't have anything on me. I always pray and believe there's a God too." She said I could see the kids on Sunday afternoon, but some other people would be there for a Bible study. I replied, "If they don't bother me, I won't bother them."

I went to her apartment on Sunday and met those people. The ladies were hugging me, and the men even tried to hug me, but I said, "Hey, even my own mother doesn't hug me…get your hands off!" I thought that they were all high.

I couldn't understand why they were so happy. I told myself that I would come back next week with some weed, and we could all get high together.

I had never known any Christians. As time went on, I knew they had something I didn't have. They had something I wanted. About four months later, I asked my wife what it was that made her so happy, and she began telling me about the Gospel of Jesus Christ.

I was trying to make myself happy by spending all my money on booze and drugs. I passed out in alleys, in bathrooms, and even in hallways of other people's houses.

Because I was using speed to stay awake, my body needed a few days of sleep to recuperate when I came down from a high. Sometimes I would pass out for three or four days.

I knew death was close. My heart would begin to race without slowing down because of all the speed I was on. I no longer took drugs because it was fun. My body required and demanded them. I was in bondage and didn't know how to get out.

empty

I wasn't happy with my life and considered killing myself. One day I was holding a gun to my head. I just sat there thinking about pulling the trigger. I wondered what would happen to my wife and children. I knew if I took my life I would end up in hell. I kept thinking there must be more to life than this.

I knew that Christians say, "Repent of your sins, and believe in the Lord, Jesus Christ." It seemed too simple. But that night I went home, fell on my knees, and cried out, "Lord, if you're real and can forgive sins, then come into my heart." That night something happened to me! I felt His cleansing touch, and I have never been the same. That was twenty-two years ago.

I called my wife and told her, "I'm saved!" She got excited and called all her relatives. Many people told her, "He's just trying to get you back."

When I visited the kids the following Sunday, my wife deliberately tried to pick a fight with me. The Lord quickened me (*by His Spirit*) and told me she was trying to see if I would fight with her. I used to hit my wife when she argued with me. I told her, "I'm sorry I ever hit you or hurt you. I'm a Christian now, and I will never hit you again."

As of this year, we have been married twenty-five years, and we have seven children. God called me into ministry soon after I was saved.

Tom Sault
Ojibwa

See Section 4.38 to see what Jesus wants to do for His followers.

unloved

When there is no one, no not one
that I can trust,
Lord God, I know that I can still
put my trust in you.
When I feel that my only friend has left
me alone,
Lord God, I know I still have a friend in you.

When I feel that my whole world has come
tumbling down,
Lord God, you are still my strong foundation.
When I am weak and defenseless,
Lord God, you are my strength and my shield.

When I feel that I have no place in this world,
Lord God, you accept me with your open
arms.
When I feel rejected by my brothers
and sisters,
Lord God, I know you are closer than
a brother.

When I am scared and so confused,
Lord God, you are my peace and confidant.
When there is no place to go,
Lord God, I find refuge in you,

When there is no one to cry to,
Lord God, I cry to you.
When all these happen to me at once,
Lord God, you are right there where you have
always been.

That is why I love you; that is why I live.

Lord, when I sing your praises, when I magnify your name, when I speak of your amazing grace, when I am me and you are you, I love you all the more. I love you even so. I love to love you…my one and only first love!

Rose Yazzie
Navajo

See Section 2.13 for the story of another person who came to know God's love.

wanted

BOOK OF HOPE

broken

After I graduated from high school, I never gave any thought to serving Jesus. I remember saying, "I will serve Jesus when I get older." I wanted to live life to the fullest without God in the picture, not realizing that was a foolish mistake.

When I was in my twenties, I wasted my life away like a prodigal son thinking life was all about drinking, trying to fit in, and being cool.

During my early thirties, God began to deal with me about eternity. Where I would spend it was my choice. I had to decide how I wanted to live. God began to take things away, the things that I had desired the most. I did not understand that my life was slipping away.

My bad drinking habits began to consume my life, but God in His love continued His pursuit of my life. Never in my whole life had I felt so helpless, and I thought no one could ever imagine how I felt.

The devil began to put thoughts of suicide in my mind, thoughts that my life was useless and that I needed to end this life of misery by taking my own life. But I cried out and called for Jesus, even though I had rejected and denied Him in my past.

I will never forget that December as long as I live. I had an encounter with my Creator, the God of the universe. I knew that I could not resist Him any longer because His love for me was so great, even during the times I hated Him. This was the day that Jesus Christ changed my life, and from that day forward, I have never been the same. He touched me and gave me life and gave me a purpose for living!

Vince Davis
Choctaw

See Section 4.57 for the story of the prodigal who came home.

healed

BOOK OF hope

lost

Adventure...thrills...excitement. Living life in the "fast lane" may seem enticing at first, but that lifestyle can *quickly* lead you down a path of destruction. My experience with nonstop partying and drinking still left me with an emptiness in my heart that I couldn't satisfy. You see, everyone has a "God-shaped hole" that only the Creator can fill. Since my God-shaped hole wasn't filled, I continued on life's fast lane. The devil tried every way he could to discourage me and even tried to kill me through a tragic car accident, but God had other plans. Because of His divine intervention, the Lord saved me from death, hell, and the grave.

A sinner lost without Christ, as the song writer wrote, "I was lost and un-done, without God or his Son, when my Savior reached down for me." God's powerful truth brings victory and freedom, so that every believer can enjoy life to its fullest potential in Him.

I believe that the unchanging Word of God is as much an answer for today as it has ever been. No matter where you are on the fast lane of life, God is waiting with open arms, ready to forgive and redeem. All you have to do is ask.

Wayne Medicine Eagle
Lakota

See Section 5.32 to learn how Jesus is the Way to the Creator.

Found

Trail of

To know the way of **hope**, you must first understand what happened when the world began. In the beginning, the Creator had a purpose in mind for everything He made. The sky, clouds, animals, earth, plants, and peoples were all given a way to live and to exist. The Creator's way of hope was for all of the creation to live in harmony. The Creator loved the first people and talked openly with them. He created them to know Him and walk in His ways.

But the first people chose not to walk with the Creator and followed a different trail. They walked away from Him. They missed the markers and lost the trail of beauty. This broke the way to the Creator. This also broke the Creator's heart!

Because of this, evil was let loose into the creation. All the peoples from all the tribes around the world have followed the wrong path ever since. And now the whole creation suffers because of this evil:

> There is no faithfulness or love in the land.
> No one recognizes me as God.
> People call down curses on others.
> They tell lies and commit murder,
> They steal and commit adultery.
> They break all my laws,
> They keep on spilling the blood of others.
> That is why the land is drying up.
> And those who live in it
> are getting weaker and weaker
> The wild animals and birds of the air are dying
> So are the fish of the ocean.
> Hosea 4:1-3 (NIRV)

Hope

From that time until now, people all over the earth have been lost. They are searching for their way back home. And because the Creator loves His children so much, He made a way for them to come back to Him. This is the message of **hope**. This is the path to peace and purpose for your life. This is the road back to the Creator.

The words of **hope** are all about finding the Creator's way once again. But maybe you have heard that if you become a follower of Jesus you must leave behind all of your Native culture. Perhaps you have been told that the Jesus Way is only a white man's religion.

Jesus came to earth because the Creator loved all people - from every tribe, clan, nation and language - and wanted to teach them how to follow the trail of **hope**. So Jesus is gathering followers from all around the world. The way of **hope** is not limited to one people or one culture. How could it be? The Creator made all people, and His plan is to bring all peoples back to Himself.

But in their attempts to find their way back home to the Creator, all the tribes and nations of the world have created their own ways to the spirit world. These attempts all fall short because they are not true to the Creator's own Way.

> God shows his anger from heaven.
> It is against all godless and evil things
> that people do. They are so evil that
> they say no to the truth.
> Romans 1:18 (NIRV)

Throughout the generations, our Native peoples have also been seeking the Creator's true identity. We have made many images of Him. We have looked for Him inside the creation. But we do not have to seek Him this way any longer. The Creator Himself came to reveal His true identity and nature to all the tribes and peoples of the world.

Trail of

In the past, God spoke to our people through the prophets. He spoke at many times. He spoke in different ways. But in these last days, he has spoken to us through his Son. He is the one whom God appointed to receive all things. God made everything through him. The Son is the gleaming brightness of God's glory. He is the exact likeness of God's being. He uses his powerful word to hold all things together. He provided the way for people to be made pure from sin.
Hebrews 1:1-3

Jesus is the Son of God who came to earth. Jesus is the One who speaks with power – His word holds the whole creation together! Jesus is the One who reveals to us the true path back to the Creator. Jesus is the Way for all Native peoples.

The Creator loves you as a Native person. He made you in His image. He wants you to walk with Him as a Native person. *The Native Book of Hope* can teach you how to love and worship the one, true Creator.

The Creator desires that all cultures of the world, including our Native Cultures, honor Him. Jesus came to make our cultures better, not take them away from us. The Creator is pleased when people from different tribes and nations worship Him. He delights when He hears many languages and sees many customs and ways of life being used to praise Him.

We must be careful not to mix the true worship of the Creator with the old religions that do not honor Him. But at the same time we must not be afraid to worship the Creator with all the unique beauty and gifts of our Native cultures that follow the Word of God.

Hope

Unfortunately, there are some people who refuse to follow the way of **hope**. Some of these people think the power of their ceremonies is greater than the power of Jesus. They serve the spirits in the old way. These spirits have refused to follow the plan of the Creator. And it is true that they have power. But let us examine the story of Jesus more closely to see how He dealt with these deceiving spirits.

When Jesus began walking among the tribes of His day, He taught the people many things. But at the core of His message was the good news that the Creator was bringing His kingdom to earth. This meant that the devil and all evil spirits that followed him were in trouble! They were about to see their strength was weak compared to the Creator's awesome power.

> Dear children, don't let anyone lead you down the wrong path. Those who do what is right are holy, just as Christ is holy. Those who do what is sinful belong to the devil. They are just like him. He has been sinning from the beginning. But the Son of God came to destroy the devil's work.
> I John 3:7-8 (NIRV)

And Jesus Christ, the Son of God, began to do just that. He healed people to take away the pain of the devil's sickness. He taught people the Creator's truth to expose the devil's lies. And because Jesus loved Native – and all – people so much, He even allowed himself to be killed. But He rose again to take away the devil's accusations against the people. This is the power that comes from walking the trail of hope. This is the power that transforms death into life.

When Jesus confronted evil spirits, they knew he was able to destroy them. Look what happened:

Trail of

> Just then a man…cried out. He was controlled by an evil spirit. He said, "What do you want with us, Jesus of Nazareth? Have you come to destroy us? I know who you are. You are the Holy One of God!" "Be quiet!" said Jesus firmly. "Come out of him!"
> The evil spirit shook the man wildly. Then it came out of him with a scream. All the people were amazed. So they asked each other. "What is this? A new teaching! And with so much authority! He gives orders to evil spirits, and they obeyed him.
> Mark 1:23-27

When Jesus came to earth, He defeated the evil spirits. He threw them out of people. He gave the evil spirits orders, and they had to obey. So on the trail of **hope**, there is no more fear of curses. Through Jesus, the Creator's way of peace and beauty can come to you in power.

> He took away the weapons of the powers and authorities. He made a public show of them. He won the battle over them by dying on the cross.
> Colossians 2:15 (NIRV)

When Jesus died on the cross, it looked like the ultimate victory for his enemies. But this was actually a great surprise by the Creator. By taking the pain and suffering caused by evil onto Himself, Jesus drained the devil and his spirits of their power. And when Jesus comes again, He will destroy these enemies forever.

Jesus' death on the cross also drained the power of sin over our lives. Jesus took away the penalty of sin for peoples all over the world. Then He rose again, so all these peoples could have a new life.

Hope

> By the power of the Holy Spirit, he was appointed to be the mighty Son of God because he rose from the dead. He is Jesus our Lord.
> Romans 1:4 (NIRV)

Today, Jesus can bring life - giving power into your life. He will bring you freedom from fear. You no longer have to be afraid of the spirits. His love for you is stronger than any curse.

Jesus will help you find purpose in your life. He will bring you into His kingdom. He will even defeat the power of darkness inside your life and change you from within. For all who receive Him, Jesus will do this.

Jesus came to make a difference. Through the trail of **hope,** your life can be changed. Jesus alone has the power to do this.

Now it is clear what your choice is. Now is the time to walk this trail of hope and never depart from it.

The Creator has chosen a path for everything He has made. He has in mind how people should live together. He does not want people to hurt themselves with drugs and alcohol. When people do not know the Way of the Creator, they do not know the proper, respectful, and loving way to treat what God has made.

As Native people we know about the pain that comes from using things and people wrongly. Maybe you know the hurt of abuse in your own life. Maybe someone has treated you wrongly. Maybe you have hurt people or misused other things in creation.

Trail of

The trail of **hope** makes it possible for this pain to be healed. And it teaches us to respect and use correctly the things God has made. The Creator teaches us how to find real love and joy with each other.

The Creator wants you to walk again on the path He has for you. On the trail of **hope**, your life can be made whole.

Many thousands of Native people have found that Jesus always keeps His promises. Now you are reading about Him and discovering His Way for yourself in this *Native Book of Hope*.

You are reading here about the life of Jesus and how He has the power to make things right. You are reading how Jesus gave the greatest gift to set Native people free. You are learning how Jesus has broken down the barriers between people and now brings them together in peace.

When you become a follower of Jesus, you can know that He will keep His promise to heal your life, too.

One day, people from every tribe and nation will live with the Creator in a new heaven and a new earth. The Creator's Word tells us:

> The time will come when the Lord will make everything new. He will send the Christ.... He must remain in heaven until the time when God makes everything new.
> Acts 3:19-21 (NIRV)

Hope

When this happens, the Creator's "way of things" will never be broken again. He will live with His people and walk with them as He did in the beginning. To share in this, you must become a follower of the Son of God - Jesus - Who said:

> "I am the way and the truth and the life. No one comes to the Father except through me."
> John 14:6 (NIRV)

How is Jesus the way to the Father? Jesus gave the gift of His life for you. His blood was poured out, and He died for you.

> We have been set free because of what Christ has done. Through his blood our sins have been forgiven. We have been set free because God's grace is so rich.
> Ephesians 1:7 (NIRV)

After Jesus died, He rose from the dead with power and glory. Now the Jesus Way of truth and life can be your way, too. When you follow the trail of **hope**, you are finding your home with the Creator.

God made us.

> He created us to belong to Christ Jesus.
> Ephesians 2:10 (NIRV)

> So then turn away from your sin. Turn to God. Then your sins will be wiped away.
> Acts 3:19 (NIRV)

Trail of

You have a real choice. You can walk on a new trail. You must turn away from your old path and turn to the Creator. Here is what you must do to become a follower of Jesus:

1. **ADMIT** to the Creator that you are captive to sin and have not followed His path for right living.

2. **BELIEVE** that the Creator of the world loves you and sent His Son Jesus to take the penalty for your sin.

3. **CONFESS** " 'Jesus is Lord.' Believe in your heart that God raised him from the dead. Then you will be saved. With your heart you believe and are made right with God. With your mouth you say Jesus is Lord. And so you are saved." Romans 10:9-10

You can tell Jesus that you will now follow the trail of **hope**:

Jesus, I believe that you died for my sins, that your blood was shed to wash away everything that I have done wrong, and that you rose again so that I can have new life. I want to turn from my sin. I want to serve and follow you. I give myself to you. Help me now to love you with all my heart and soul and mind. I commit my future to you. Jesus, become Lord of my life. Guide me by your Holy Spirit along the trail of **hope.** Amen.

> God's grace has saved you
> because of your faith in Christ.
> Your salvation doesn't
> come from anything you do.
> It is God's gift.
> Ephesians 2:8 (NIRV)

Hope

The Creator wants you to have the fullest life possible. Here are some important steps for you to take on this new path as a follower of Jesus.

READ God's word every day
The Bible provides for our daily spiritual nourishment on the trail of **hope**. It teaches us about the Creator and how He wants us to live. There is more than enough for a lifetime of learning and growing.

PRAY Heart to Heart with God
Prayer is your lifeline to the Creator. Prayer is you talking to God and God's talking to you. God not only hears our prayers, but also answers them. He delights in listening to you. You are never alone no matter what struggles or problems you may face. Pour out your heart to Him; our Creator can do more than you can ask or imagine.

GATHER Meeting with other followers of Jesus
As we learn the new path from our Creator, we can be encouraged and strengthened by meeting together weekly for prayer, Bible study, and worship.

STORYTELLING Telling others about your personal story on the trail of **hope**
You too are a "storyteller" for Jesus. His path is for all people from every tribe, nation, clan and tongue. The honor of helping others discover this path has been given to you.
Matthew 28:18-20

thank you!

The *Native Book of Hope* shows: why Jesus was willing to give the greatest gift ever given to bring all Native people back to the Creator; how the power of Jesus is able to overcome evil spirits, fear, diseases and even death; and how you can find peace, purpose, and power for your life by following the trail of hope.

There are no words that can begin to say "Thank You" to the Creator for the trail of hope that He has given us to follow. If we possessed all the riches of this world, we could never begin to repay God for the love He has shown us in these stories of Hope and the Gospel of Hope that follows.

Our hands go out to those of you whose journey has brought you to the Book of Hope. For many, this junction in your travels is a welcomed sign giving you the direction you need to complete the circle of life back to the Creator. For others, you have now come to the crossroads, and your life hangs in the balance. We say "Thank You" to Jesus for helping us make the trail of hope our path for life.

This book tells the story of the Creator's love for all people.

Read it and find His love for you.

BOOK OF hope

1 The Thirty Years of Preparation

1.1 Introduction

This is the good news about Jesus Christ, the Son of God.[1]

Many people have tried to tell the story of what God has done among us. They wrote what we had been told by the ones who were there in the beginning and saw what happened. So I made a careful study of everything and then decided to write and tell you exactly what took place. Honorable Theophilus, I have done this to let you know the truth about what you have heard.[2]

In the beginning was the one who is called the Word.
    The Word was with God and was truly God.
From the very beginning the Word was with God.
And with this Word, God created all things.
    Nothing was made without the Word.
Everything that was created received its life from him,
    and his life gave light to everyone.
The light keeps shining in the dark,
    and darkness has never put it out.
God sent a man named John,
who came to tell about the light
    and to lead all people to have faith.
John wasn't that light.
    He came only to tell about the light.

The true light that shines on everyone
    was coming into the world.
The Word was in the world,
but no one knew him,
    though God had made the world with his Word.
He came into his own world,
    but his own nation did not welcome him.
Yet some people accepted him and put their faith in him.
    So he gave them the right to be the children of God.
They were not God's children by nature

or because of any human desires.
God himself was the one who made them his children.

The Word became a human being and lived here with us.
We saw his true glory,
   the glory of the only Son of the Father.
From him all the kindness and all the truth of God
   have come down to us.

John spoke about him and shouted, "This is the one I told you would come! He is greater than I am, because he was alive before I was born."

Because of all that the Son is, we have been given one blessing after another. The Law was given by Moses, but Jesus Christ brought us undeserved kindness and truth. No one has ever seen God. The only Son, who is truly God and is closest to the Father, has shown us what God is like.[3]

1.2 The Birth of John the Baptist Foretold

When Herod was king of Judea, there was a priest by the name of Zechariah from the priestly group of Abijah. His wife Elizabeth was from the family of Aaron. Both of them were good people and pleased the Lord God by obeying all that he had commanded. But they did not have children. Elizabeth could not have any, and both Zechariah and Elizabeth were already old.

One day Zechariah's group of priests were on duty, and he was serving God as a priest. According to the custom of the priests, he had been chosen to go into the Lord's temple that day and to burn incense, while the people stood outside praying.

All at once an angel from the Lord appeared to Zechariah at the right side of the altar. Zechariah was confused and afraid when he saw the angel. But the angel told him:

> Don't be afraid, Zechariah! God has heard your prayers. Your wife Elizabeth will have a son, and you must name him John. His birth will make you very happy, and many people will be glad. Your son will be a great servant of the Lord. He must never drink wine or beer, and the power of the Holy Spirit will be with him from the time he is born. John will lead many people in Israel to turn back to the Lord their God. He will go ahead of the Lord with the same power and spirit that Elijah had. And because of John, parents will be more thoughtful of their children. And people who now disobey God will begin to think as they ought to. That is how John will get people ready for the Lord.

Zechariah said to the angel, "How will I know this is going to happen? My wife and I are both very old."

The angel answered, "I am Gabriel, God's servant, and I was sent to tell you this good news. You have not believed what I have said. So you will not be able to say a thing until all this happens. But everything will take place when it is supposed to."

The crowd was waiting for Zechariah and kept wondering why he was staying so long in the temple. When he did come out, he could not speak, and they knew he had seen a vision. He motioned to them with his hands, but did not say a thing.

When Zechariah's time of service in the temple was over, he went home. Soon after that, his wife was expecting a baby, and for five months she did not leave the house. She said to herself, "What the Lord has done for me will keep people from looking down on me."

1.3 The Birth of Jesus Foretold

One month later God sent the angel Gabriel to the town of Nazareth in Galilee with a message for a virgin named Mary. She was engaged to Joseph from the family of King David. The angel greeted Mary and said, "You are truly blessed! The Lord is with you."

Mary was confused by the angel's words and wondered what they meant. Then the angel told Mary, "Don't be afraid! God is pleased with you, and you will have a son. His name will be Jesus. He will be great and will be called the Son of God Most High. The Lord God will make him king, as his ancestor David was. He will rule the people of Israel forever, and his kingdom will never end."

Mary asked the angel, "How can this happen? I am not married!"

The angel answered, "The Holy Spirit will come down to you, and God's power will come over you. So your child will be called the holy Son of God. Your relative Elizabeth is also going to have a son, even though she is old. No one thought she could ever have a baby, but in three months she will have a son. Nothing is impossible for God!"

Mary said, "I am the Lord's servant! Let it happen as you have said." And the angel left her.

1.4 Mary Visits Elizabeth

A short time later Mary hurried to a town in the hill country of Judea. She went into Zechariah's home, where she greeted Elizabeth. When Elizabeth heard Mary's greeting, her baby moved within her.

The Holy Spirit came upon Elizabeth. Then in a loud voice she said to Mary:

God has blessed you more than any other woman! He has also blessed the child you will have. Why should the mother of my Lord come to me? As soon as I heard your greeting, my baby became happy and moved within me. The Lord has blessed you because you believed that he will keep his promise.

1.5 Mary's Song

Mary said:

With all my heart I praise the Lord,
  and I am glad because of God my Savior.
He cares for me, his humble servant.
From now on, all people will say
  God has blessed me.
God All-Powerful has done great things for me,
  and his name is holy.
He always shows mercy
  to everyone who worships him.
The Lord has used his powerful arm
  to scatter those who are proud.
He drags strong rulers from their thrones
  and puts humble people in places of power.
God gives the hungry good things to eat,
  and sends the rich away with nothing.
He helps his servant Israel
  and is always merciful to his people.
The Lord made this promise to our ancestors,
  to Abraham and his family forever!

Mary stayed with Elizabeth about three months. Then she went back home.

1.6 The Birth of John the Baptist

When Elizabeth's son was born, her neighbors and relatives heard how kind the Lord had been to her, and they too were glad.

Eight days later they did for the child what the Law of Moses commands. They were going to name him Zechariah, after his father. But Elizabeth said, "No! His name is John."

The people argued, "No one in your family has ever been named John." So they motioned to Zechariah to find out what he wanted to name his son.

Zechariah asked for a writing tablet. Then he wrote, "His name is John." Everyone was amazed. Right away, Zechariah started speaking and praising God.

All the neighbors were frightened because of what had happened, and everywhere in the hill country people kept talking about these things. Everyone who heard about this wondered what this child would grow up to be. They knew that the Lord was with him.

1.7 Zechariah Praises the Lord

The Holy Spirit came upon Zechariah, and he began to speak:

Praise the Lord, the God of Israel!
    He has come to save his people.
Our God has given us a mighty Savior
    from the family of David his servant.
Long ago the Lord promised
    by the words of his holy prophets
To save us from our enemies
    and from everyone who hates us.
God said he would be kind to our people
    and keep his sacred promise.
He told our ancestor Abraham
    that he would rescue us from our enemies.
Then we could serve him without fear,
    by being holy and good as long as we live.

You, my son, will be called
    a prophet of God in heaven above.
You will go ahead of the Lord
    to get everything ready for him.
You will tell his people
    that they can be saved when their sins are forgiven.
God's love and kindness will shine upon us
    like the sun that rises in the sky.
On us who live in the dark shadow of death
this light will shine
    to guide us into a life of peace.

As John grew up, God's Spirit gave him great power. John lived in the desert until the time he was sent to the people of Israel.[6]

1.8 The Birth of Jesus

This is how Jesus Christ was born. A young woman named Mary was engaged to Joseph from King David's family. But before they were married, she learned that she was going to have a baby by God's Holy Spirit. Joseph was a good man and did not want to embarrass Mary in front of everyone. So he decided to quietly call off the wedding.

While Joseph was thinking about this, an angel from the Lord came to him in a dream. The angel said, "Joseph, the baby that Mary will have is from the Holy Spirit. Go ahead and marry her. Then after her baby is born, name him Jesus, because he will save his people from their sins."

So the Lord's promise came true, just as the prophet had said, "A virgin will have a baby boy, and he will be called Immanuel," which means "God is with us."

After Joseph woke up, he and Mary were soon married, just as the Lord's angel had told him to do. But they did not sleep together before her baby was born.[5]

About that time Emperor Augustus gave orders for the names of all the people to be listed in record books. These first records were made when Quirinius was governor of Syria.

Everyone had to go to their own hometown to be listed. So Joseph had to leave Nazareth in Galilee and go to Bethlehem in Judea. Long ago Bethlehem had been King David's hometown, and Joseph went there because he was from David's family.

Mary was engaged to Joseph and traveled with him to Bethlehem. She was soon going to have a baby, and while they were there, she gave birth to her first-born son. She dressed him in baby clothes and laid him on a bed of hay, because there was no room for them in the inn.

1.9 The Shepherds and the Angels

That night in the fields near Bethlehem some shepherds were guarding their sheep. All at once an angel came down to them from the Lord, and the brightness of the Lord's glory flashed around them. The shepherds were frightened. But the angel said, "Don't be afraid! I have good news for you, which will make everyone happy. This very day in King David's hometown a Savior was born for you. He is Christ the Lord. You will know who he is, because you will find him dressed in baby clothes and lying on a bed of hay."

Suddenly many other angels came down from heaven and joined in praising God. They said:

"Praise God in heaven!
Peace on earth to everyone who pleases God."

After the angels had left and gone back to heaven, the shepherds said to each other, "Let's go to Bethlehem and see what the Lord has told us about." They hurried off and found Mary and Joseph, and they saw the baby lying on a bed of hay.

When the shepherds saw Jesus, they told his parents what the angel had said about him. Everyone listened and was surprised. But Mary kept thinking about all this and wondering what it meant.

As the shepherds returned to their sheep, they were praising God and saying wonderful things about him. Everything they had seen and heard was just as the angel had said.

Eight days later Jesus' parents did for him what the Law of Moses commands. And they named him Jesus, just as the angel had told Mary when he promised she would have a baby.

1.10 Jesus Presented in the Temple

The time came for Mary and Joseph to do what the Law of Moses says a mother is supposed to do after her baby is born.

They took Jesus to the temple in Jerusalem and presented him to the Lord, just as the Law of the Lord says, "Each first-born baby boy belongs to the Lord." The Law of the Lord also says that parents have to offer a sacrifice, giving at least a pair of doves or two young pigeons. So that is what Mary and Joseph did.

At this time a man named Simeon was living in Jerusalem. Simeon was a good man. He loved God and was waiting for God to save the people of Israel. God's Spirit came to him and told him that he would not die until he had seen Christ the Lord.

When Mary and Joseph brought Jesus to the temple to do what the Law of Moses says should be done for a new baby, the Spirit told Simeon to go into the temple. Simeon took the baby Jesus in his arms and praised God,

"Lord, I am your servant,
and now I can die in peace,
　　because you have kept your promise to me.
With my own eyes I have seen
what you have done to save your people,
　　and foreign nations will also see this.

Your mighty power is a light for all nations,
 and it will bring honor to your people Israel."

Jesus' parents were surprised at what Simeon had said. Then he blessed them and told Mary, "This child of yours will cause many people in Israel to fall and others to stand. The child will be like a warning sign. Many people will reject him, and you, Mary, will suffer as though you had been stabbed by a dagger. But all this will show what people are really thinking."

The prophet Anna was also there in the temple. She was the daughter of Phanuel from the tribe of Asher, and she was very old. In her youth she had been married for seven years, but her husband died. And now she was eighty-four years old. Night and day she served God in the temple by praying and often going without eating.

At that time Anna came in and praised God. She spoke about the child Jesus to everyone who hoped for Jerusalem to be set free.[6]

1.11 The Visit of the Wise Men

When Jesus was born in the village of Bethlehem in Judea, Herod was king. During this time some wise men from the east came to Jerusalem and said, "Where is the child born to be king of the Jews? We saw his star in the east and have come to worship him."

When King Herod heard about this, he was worried, and so was everyone else in Jerusalem. Herod brought together the chief priests and the teachers of the Law of Moses and asked them, "Where will the Messiah be born?"

They told him, "He will be born in Bethlehem, just as the prophet wrote,

'Bethlehem in the land of Judea,
 you are very important among the towns of Judea.
From your town will come a leader,
 who will be like a shepherd for my people Israel.' "

Herod secretly called in the wise men and asked them when they had first seen the star. He told them, "Go to Bethlehem and search carefully for the child. As soon as you find him, let me know. I want to go and worship him too."

The wise men listened to what the king said and then left. And the star they had seen in the east went on ahead of them until it stopped over the place where the child was. They were thrilled and excited to see the star.

When the men went into the house and saw the child with Mary, his mother, they knelt down and worshiped him. They took out their gifts of gold, frankincense, and myrrh and gave them to him. Later they were warned in a dream not to return to Herod, and they went back home by another road.

1.12 The Escape to Egypt

After the wise men had gone, an angel from the Lord appeared to Joseph in a dream and said, "Get up! Hurry and take the child and his mother to Egypt! Stay there until I tell you to return, because Herod is looking for the child and wants to kill him."

That night, Joseph got up and took his wife and the child to Egypt, where they stayed until Herod died. So the Lord's promise came true, just as the prophet had said, "I called my son out of Egypt."

1.13 The Killing of the Children

When Herod found out that the wise men from the east had tricked him, he was very angry. He gave orders for his men to kill all the boys who lived in or near Bethlehem and were two years old and younger. This was based on what he had learned from the wise men.

So the Lord's promise came true, just as the prophet Jeremiah had said,

"In Ramah a voice was heard
  crying and weeping loudly.
Rachel was mourning for her children,
and she refused to be comforted,
  because they were dead."

1.14 The Return to Nazareth

After King Herod died, an angel from the Lord appeared in a dream to Joseph while he was still in Egypt. The angel said, "Get up and take the child and his mother back to Israel. The people who wanted to kill him are now dead."

Joseph got up and left with them for Israel. But when he heard that Herod's son Archelaus was now ruler of Judea, he was afraid to go there. Then in a dream he was told to go to Galilee, and they went to live there in the town of Nazareth. So the Lord's promise came true, just as the prophet had said, "He will be called a Nazarene." [7]

The child Jesus grew. He became strong and wise, and God blessed him.

1.15 The Boy Jesus at the Temple

Every year Jesus' parents went to Jerusalem for Passover. And when Jesus was twelve years old, they all went there as usual for the celebration. After Passover his parents left, but they did not know that Jesus had stayed on in the city. They thought he was traveling with some other people, and they went a whole day before they started looking for him. When they could not find him with their relatives and friends, they went back to Jerusalem and started looking for him there.

Three days later they found Jesus sitting in the temple, listening to the teachers and asking them questions. Everyone who heard him was surprised at how much he knew and at the answers he gave.

When his parents found him, they were amazed. His mother said, "Son, why have you done this to us? Your father and I have been very worried, and we have been searching for you!"

Jesus answered, "Why did you have to look for me? Didn't you know that I would be in my Father's house?" But they did not understand what he meant.

Jesus went back to Nazareth with his parents and obeyed them. His mother kept on thinking about all that had happened.

Jesus became wise, and he grew strong. God was pleased with him and so were the people.

> "We are of the same opinion with the people of the United States; You consider yourselves as independent people; We, as the original inhabitants of this country, and sovereigns of the soil, look upon ourselves as equally independent, and free as any other nation or nations"
>
> **Joseph Brant "Tyendinaga" Mohawk 1784**

REVIEW QUESTIONS, SECTION I

1. Jesus came into the world to give to all those who _____ Him and put their_____ Him the right to become _____ of _____. (1.1)

2. The law was given through Moses. but _____ _____ and _____ came through Jesus Christ. (1.1)

3. What was the good news the angel of the Lord gave the shepherds? "This very day in King David's hometown a _____ was born for you. He is Christ the Lord." (1.9)

4. The elderly man Simeon said, "With my own eyes I have seen what You have done to _____ Your people." (1.10)

5. The wise men came from the east to _____ the newborn king of the Jews. (1.11)

6. Jesus became _____ and He grew_____. God was _____ with Him and so were the _____. (1.15)

2 The Year of Inauguration

2.1 John the Baptist Prepares the Way

For fifteen years Emperor Tiberius had ruled that part of the world. Pontius Pilate was governor of Judea, and Herod was the ruler of Galilee. Herod's brother, Philip, was the ruler in the countries of Iturea and Trachonitis, and Lysanias was the ruler of Abilene. Annas and Caiaphas were the Jewish high priests.

At that time God spoke to Zechariah's son John, who was living in the desert. So John went along the Jordan Valley, telling the people, "Turn back to God and be baptized! Then your sins will be forgiven." Isaiah the prophet wrote about John when he said,

> "In the desert someone is shouting,
> 'Get the road ready for the Lord!
>   Make a straight path for him.
> Fill up every valley and level every mountain and hill.
> Straighten the crooked paths
>   and smooth out the rough roads.
> Then everyone will see the saving power of God.' " [8]

John wore clothes made of camel's hair. He had a leather strap around his waist and ate grasshoppers and wild honey.

From Jerusalem and all Judea and from the Jordan River Valley crowds of people went to John. They told how sorry they were for their sins, and he baptized them in the river.

Many Pharisees and Sadducees also came to be baptized. But John said to them:

> You bunch of snakes! Who warned you to run from the coming judgment? Do something to show that you have really given up your sins. And don't start telling yourselves that you belong to Abraham's family. I tell you that God can turn these stones into children for Abraham. An ax is ready to cut the trees down at their roots. Any tree that doesn't produce good fruit will be chopped down and thrown into a fire." [9]

The crowds asked John, "What should we do?"

John told them, "If you have two coats, give one to someone who doesn't have any. If you have food, share it with someone else."

When tax collectors came to be baptized, they asked John, "Teacher, what should we do?"

John told them, "Don't make people pay more than they owe."

Some soldiers asked him, "And what about us? What do we have to do?"

John told them, "Don't force people to pay money to make you leave them alone. Be satisfied with your pay."

Everyone became excited and wondered, "Could John be the Messiah?"

John said, "I am just baptizing with water. But someone more powerful is going to come, and I am not good enough even to untie his sandals. He will baptize you with the Holy Spirit and with fire. His threshing fork is in his hand, and he is ready to separate the wheat from the husks. He will store the wheat in his barn and burn the husks with a fire that never goes out."

In many different ways John preached the good news to the people.[10]

2.2 The Baptism of Jesus

Jesus left Galilee and went to the Jordan River to be baptized by John. But John kept objecting and said, "I ought to be baptized by you. Why have you come to me?"

Jesus answered, "For now this is how it should be, because we must do all that God wants us to do." Then John agreed.

So Jesus was baptized. And as soon as he came out of the water, the sky opened, and he saw the Spirit of God coming down on him like a dove. Then a voice from heaven said, "This is my own dear Son, and I am pleased with him." [11]

When Jesus began to preach, he was about thirty years old. [12]

2.3 The Temptation of Jesus

The Holy Spirit led Jesus into the desert, so that the devil could test him. After Jesus had gone without eating for forty days and nights, he was very hungry. Then the devil came to him and said, "If you are God's Son, tell these stones to turn into bread."

Jesus answered, "The Scriptures say:

'No one can live only on food.
People need every word that God has spoken.' "

Next, the devil took Jesus to the holy city and had him stand on the highest part of the temple. The devil said, "If you are God's Son, jump off. The Scriptures say:

'God will give his angels orders about you.
They will catch you in their arms,
and you won't hurt your feet on the stones.' "

Jesus answered, "The Scriptures also say, 'Don't try to test the Lord your God!' "

Finally, the devil took Jesus up on a very high mountain and showed him all the kingdoms on earth and their power. The devil said to him, "I will give all this to you, if you will bow down and worship me."

Jesus answered, "Go away Satan! The Scriptures say:

'Worship the Lord your God
and serve only him.' "

Then the devil left Jesus, and angels came to help him. [13]

2.4 John the Baptist Denies Being the Messiah

The Jewish leaders in Jerusalem sent priests and temple helpers to ask John who he was. He told them plainly, "I am not the Messiah." Then when they asked him if he were Elijah, he said, "No, I am not!" And when they asked if he were the Prophet, he also said "No!"

Finally, they said, "Who are you then? We have to give an answer to the ones who sent us. Tell us who you are!"

John answered in the words of the prophet Isaiah, "I am only someone shouting in the desert, 'Get the road ready for the Lord!' "

Some Pharisees had also been sent to John. They asked him, "Why are you baptizing people, if you are not the Messiah or Elijah or the Prophet?"

John told them, "I use water to baptize people. But here with you is someone you don't know. Even though I came first, I am not good enough to untie his sandals." John said this as he was baptizing east of the Jordan River in Bethany.

2.5 Jesus the Lamb of God

The next day, John saw Jesus coming toward him and said:
Here is the Lamb of God who takes away the sin of the world! He is the one I told you about when I said, 'Someone else will come. He is greater than I am, because he was alive before I was born.' I didn't know who he was. But I came to baptize you with water, so that everyone in Israel would see him.

I was there and saw the Spirit come down on him like a dove from heaven. And the Spirit stayed on him. Before this I didn't know who he was. But the one who sent me to baptize with water had told me, 'You will see the Spirit come down and stay on someone. Then you will know that he is the one who will baptize with the Holy Spirit.' I saw this happen, and I tell you that he is the Son of God.

2.6 Jesus' First Disciples

The next day, John was there again, and two of his followers were with him. When he saw Jesus walking by, he said, "Here is the Lamb of God!" John's two followers heard him, and they went with Jesus.

When Jesus turned and saw them, he asked, "What do you want?"

They answered, "Rabbi, where do you live?" The Hebrew word "Rabbi" means "Teacher."

Jesus replied, "Come and see!" It was already about four o'clock in the afternoon when they went with him and saw where he lived. So they stayed on for the rest of the day.

One of the two men who had heard John and had gone with Jesus was Andrew, the brother of Simon Peter. The first thing Andrew did was to find his brother and tell him, "We have found the Messiah!" The Hebrew word "Messiah" means the same as the Greek word "Christ."

Andrew brought his brother to Jesus. And when Jesus saw him, he said, "Simon son of John, you will be called Cephas." This name can be translated as "Peter."

2.7 Jesus Calls Phillip and Nathanael

The next day Jesus decided to go to Galilee. There he met Philip, who was from Bethsaida, the hometown of Andrew and Peter. Jesus said to Philip, "Come with me."

Philip then found Nathanael and said, "We have found the one that Moses and the Prophets wrote about. He is Jesus, the son of Joseph from Nazareth."

Nathanael asked, "Can anything good come from Nazareth?"

Philip answered, "Come and see."

When Jesus saw Nathanael coming toward him, he said, "Here is a true descendant of our ancestor Israel. And he isn't deceitful."

"How do you know me?" Nathanael asked.

Jesus answered, "Before Philip called you, I saw you under the fig tree."

Nathanael said, "Rabbi, you are the Son of God and the King of Israel!"

Jesus answered, "Did you believe me just because I said that I saw you under the fig tree? You will see something even greater. I tell you for certain that you will see heaven open and God's angels going up and coming down on the Son of Man."

2.8 Jesus Changes Water to Wine

Three days later Mary, the mother of Jesus, was at a wedding feast in the village of Cana in Galilee. Jesus and his disciples had also been invited and were there.

When the wine was all gone, Mary said to Jesus, "They don't have any more wine."

Jesus replied, "Mother, my time hasn't yet come! You must not tell me what to do."

Mary then said to the servants, "Do whatever Jesus tells you to do."

At the feast there were six stone water jars that were used by the people for washing themselves in the way that their religion said they must. Each jar held about twenty or thirty gallons. Jesus told the servants to fill them to the top with water. Then after the jars had been filled, he said, "Now take some water and give it to the man in charge of the feast."

The servants did as Jesus told them, and the man in charge drank some of the water that had now turned into wine. He did not know where the wine had come from, but the servants did. He called the bridegroom over and said, "The best wine is always served first. Then after the guests have had plenty, the other wine is served. But you have kept the best until last!"

This was Jesus' first miracle, and he did it in the village of Cana in Galilee. There Jesus showed his glory, and his disciples put their faith in him. After this, he went with his mother, his brothers, and his disciples to the town of Capernaum, where they stayed for a few days.

2.9 Jesus Clears the Temple

Not long before the Jewish festival of Passover, Jesus went to Jerusalem. There he found people selling cattle, sheep, and doves in the temple. He also saw money-changers sitting at their tables. So he took some rope and made a whip. Then he chased everyone out of the temple, together with their sheep and cattle. He turned over the tables of the moneychangers and scattered their coins.

Jesus said to the people who had been selling doves, "Get those doves out of here! Don't make my Father's house a marketplace."

The disciples then remembered that the Scriptures say, "My love for your house burns in me like a fire."

The Jewish leaders asked Jesus, "What miracle will you work to show us why you have done this?"

"Destroy this temple," Jesus answered, "and in three days I will build it again!"

The leaders replied, "It took forty-six years to build this temple. What makes you think you can rebuild it in three days?"

But Jesus was talking about his body as a temple. And when he was raised from death, his disciples remembered what he had told them. Then they believed the Scriptures and the words of Jesus.

In Jerusalem during Passover many people put their faith in Jesus, because they saw him work miracles. But Jesus knew what was in their hearts, and he would not let them have power over him. No one had to tell him what people were like. He already knew.

2.10 Jesus Teaches Nicodemus

There was a man named Nicodemus who was a Pharisee and a Jewish leader. One night he went to Jesus and said, "Sir, we know that God has sent you to teach us. You could not work these miracles, unless God were with you."

Jesus replied, "I tell you for certain that you must be born from above before you can see God's kingdom!"

Nicodemus asked, "How can a grown man ever be born a second time?" Jesus answered:

> I tell you for certain that before you can get into God's kingdom, you must be born not only by water, but by the Spirit. Humans give life to their children. Yet only God's Spirit can change you into a child of God. Don't be surprised when I say that you must be born from above. Only God's Spirit gives new life. The Spirit is like

the wind that blows wherever it wants to. You can hear the wind, but you don't know where it comes from or where it is going.

"How can this be?" Nicodemus asked.

Jesus replied:

> How can you be a teacher of Israel and not know these things? I tell you for certain that we know what we are talking about because we have seen it ourselves. But none of you will accept what we say. If you don't believe when I talk to you about things on earth, how can you possibly believe if I talk to you about things in heaven?
>
> No one has gone up to heaven except the Son of Man, who came down from there. And the Son of Man must be lifted up, just as that metal snake was lifted up by Moses in the desert. Then everyone who has faith in the Son of Man will have eternal life.
>
> God loved the people of this world so much that he gave his only Son, so that everyone who has faith in him will have eternal life and never really die. God did not send his Son into the world to condemn its people. He sent him to save them! No one who has faith in God's Son will be condemned. But everyone who doesn't have faith in him has already been condemned for not having faith in God's only Son.
>
> The light has come into the world, and people who do evil things are judged guilty because they love the dark more than the light. People who do evil hate the light and won't come to the light, because it clearly shows what they have done. But everyone who lives by the truth will come to the light, because they want others to know that God is really the one doing what they do.

2.11 John the Baptist's Testimony About Jesus

Later, Jesus and his disciples went to Judea, where he stayed with them for a while and was baptizing people.

John had not yet been put in jail. He was at Aenon near Salim, where there was a lot of water, and people were coming there for John to baptize them.

John's followers got into an argument with a Jewish man about a ceremony of washing. They went to John and said, "Rabbi, you spoke about a man when you were with him east of the Jordan. He is now baptizing people, and everyone is going to him."

John replied:

> No one can do anything unless God in heaven allows it. You surely remember how I told you that 'I am not the Messiah. I am

only the one sent ahead of him.' At a wedding the groom is the one who gets married. The best man is glad just to be there and to hear the groom's voice. That's why I am so glad. Jesus must become more important, while I become less important.

God's Son comes from heaven and is above all others. Everyone who comes from the earth belongs to the earth and speaks about earthly things. The one who comes from heaven is above all others. He speaks about what he has seen and heard, and yet no one believes him. But everyone who does believe him has shown that God is truthful. The Son was sent to speak God's message, and he has been given the full power of God's Spirit.

The Father loves the Son and has given him everything. Everyone who has faith in the Son has eternal life. But no one who rejects him will ever share in that life, and God will be angry with them forever.

Jesus knew that the Pharisees had heard that he was winning and baptizing more followers than John was. But Jesus' disciples were really the ones doing the baptizing, and not Jesus himself.

Jesus left Judea and started for Galilee again. [14]

2.12 Imprisonment of John the Baptist

But to Herod the ruler, John said, "It was wrong for you to take Herodias, your brother's wife." John also said that Herod had done many other bad things. Finally, Herod put John in jail, and this was the worst thing he had done. [15]

When Jesus heard that John had been put in prison, [16] he returned to Galilee with the power of the Spirit. [17]

2.13 Jesus Talks with a Samaritan Woman

This time Jesus had to go through Samaria, and on his way he came to the town of Sychar. It was near the field that Jacob had long ago given to his son Joseph. The well that Jacob had dug was still there, and Jesus sat down beside it because he was tired from traveling. It was noon, and after Jesus' disciples had gone into town to buy some food, a Samaritan woman came to draw water from the well.

Jesus asked her, "Would you please give me a drink of water?"

"You are a Jew," she replied, "and I am a Samaritan woman. How can you ask me for a drink of water when Jews and Samaritans won't have anything to do with each other?"

Jesus answered, "You don't know what God wants to give you, and you don't know who is asking you for a drink. If you did, you would ask me for the water that gives life."

"Sir," the woman said, "you don't even have a bucket, and the well is deep. Where are you going to get this life-giving water? Our ancestor Jacob dug this well for us, and his family and animals got water from it. Are you greater than Jacob?"

Jesus answered, "Everyone who drinks this water will get thirsty again. But no one who drinks the water I give will ever be thirsty again. The water I give is like a flowing fountain that gives eternal life."

The woman replied, "Sir, please give me a drink of that water! Then I won't get thirsty and have to come to this well again."

Jesus told her, "Go and bring your husband."

The woman answered, "I don't have a husband."

"That's right," Jesus replied, "you're telling the truth. You don't have a husband. You have already been married five times, and the man you are now living with isn't your husband."

The woman said, "Sir, I can see that you are a prophet. My ancestors worshiped on this mountain, but you Jews say Jerusalem is the only place to worship."

Jesus said to her: "Believe me, the time is coming when you won't worship the Father either on this mountain or in Jerusalem. You Samaritans don't really know the one you worship. But we Jews do know the God we worship, and by using us, God will save the world. But a time is coming, and it is already here! Even now the true worshipers are being led by the Spirit to worship the Father according to the truth. These are the ones the Father is seeking to worship him. God is Spirit, and those who worship God must be led by the Spirit to worship him according to the truth."

The woman said, "I know that the Messiah will come. He is the one we call Christ. When he comes, he will explain everything to us."

"I am that one," Jesus told her, "and I am speaking to you now."

2.14 The Disciples Rejoin Jesus

The disciples returned about this time and were surprised to find Jesus talking with a woman. But none of them asked him what he wanted or why he was talking with her.

The woman left her water jar and ran back into town. She said to the people, "Come and see a man who told me everything I have ever done! Could he be the Messiah?" Everyone in town went out to see Jesus.

While this was happening, Jesus' disciples were saying to him, "Teacher, please eat something."

But Jesus told them, "I have food that you don't know anything about."

His disciples started asking each other, "Has someone brought him something to eat?"

Jesus said:

My food is to do what God wants! He is the one who sent me, and I must finish the work that he gave me to do. You may say that there are still four months until harvest time. But I tell you to look, and you will see that the fields are ripe and ready to harvest.

Even now the harvest workers are receiving their reward by gathering a harvest that brings eternal life. Then everyone who planted the seed and everyone who harvests the crop will celebrate together. So the saying proves true, "Some plant the seed, and others harvest the crop." I am sending you to harvest crops in fields where others have done all the hard work.

2.15 Many Samaritans Believe

A lot of Samaritans in that town put their faith in Jesus because the woman had said, "This man told me everything I have ever done." They came and asked him to stay in their town, and he stayed on for two days.

Many more Samaritans put their faith in Jesus because of what they heard him say. They told the woman, "We no longer have faith in Jesus just because of what you told us. We have heard him ourselves, and we are certain that he is the Savior of the world!"

2.16 Jesus Returns to Galilee

Jesus had said, "Prophets are honored everywhere, except in their own country." Then two days later he left and went to Galilee. The people there welcomed him, because they had gone to the festival in Jerusalem and had seen everything he had done.

2.17 Jesus Heals an Official's Son

While Jesus was in Galilee, he returned to the village of Cana, where he had turned the water into wine. There was an official in Capernaum whose son was sick. And when the man heard that Jesus had come from Judea, he went and begged him to keep his son from dying.

Jesus told the official, "You won't have faith unless you see miracles and wonders!"

The man replied, "Lord, please come before my son dies!"

Jesus then said, "Your son will live. Go on home to him." The man believed Jesus and started back home.

Some of the official's servants met him along the road and told him, "Your son is better!" He asked them when the boy got better, and they answered, "The fever left him yesterday at one o'clock."

The boy's father realized that at one o'clock the day before, Jesus had told him, "Your son will live!" So the man and everyone in his family put their faith in Jesus.

This was the second miracle that Jesus worked after he left Judea and went to Galilee. [18]

2.18 Jesus Rejected at Nazareth

Jesus went back to Nazareth, where he had been brought up, and as usual he went to the meeting place on the Sabbath. When he stood up to read from the Scriptures, he was given the book of Isaiah the prophet. He opened it and read,

"The Lord's Spirit has come to me,
because he has chosen me
 to tell the good news to the poor.
The Lord has sent me to announce freedom
for prisoners, to give sight to the blind,
to free everyone who suffers,
 and to say, 'This is the year the Lord has chosen.' "

Jesus closed the book, then handed it back to the man in charge and sat down. Everyone in the meeting place looked straight at Jesus.

Then Jesus said to them, "What you have just heard me read has come true today."

All the people started talking about Jesus and were amazed at the wonderful things he said. They kept on asking, "Isn't he Joseph's son?"

Jesus answered:

You will certainly want to tell me this saying, "Doctor, first make yourself well." You will tell me to do the same things here in my own hometown that you heard I did in Capernaum. But you can be sure that no prophets are liked by the people of their own hometown.

Once during the time of Elijah there was no rain for three and a half years, and people everywhere were starving. There were many widows in Israel, but Elijah was sent only to a widow in the town of Zarephath near the city of Sidon. During the time of the prophet Elisha, many men in Israel had leprosy. But no one was healed, except Naaman who lived in Syria.

When the people in the meeting place heard Jesus say this, they became so angry that they got up and threw him out of town. They dragged him to the edge of the cliff on which the town was built, because they wanted to throw him down from there. But Jesus slipped through the crowd and got away. [19]

2.19 Jesus Begins to Preach

But instead of staying in Nazareth, Jesus moved to Capernaum. This town was beside Lake Galilee in the territory of Zebulun and Naphtali. So God's promise came true, just as the prophet Isaiah had said,

"Listen, lands of Zebulun and Naphtali,
  lands along the road to the sea
  and east of the Jordan!
Listen Galilee, land of the Gentiles!
Although your people live in darkness,
  they will see a bright light.
Although they live in the shadow of death,
  a light will shine on them."

Then Jesus started preaching [20] the good news that comes from God. He said, "The time has come! God's kingdom will soon be here. Turn back to God and believe the good news!"[21] News about him spread everywhere. He taught in the Jewish meeting places, and everyone praised him. [22]

> We who are clay blended by the Master Potter, come from the kiln of Creation in many hues. How can people say one skin is colored, when each has its own coloration? What should it matter that one bowl is dark and the other pale, if each is of good design and serves its purpose well."
> **Polingaysi Qoyawayma, Hopi**

REVIEW QUESTIONS, SECTION 2

1. John the Baptist told the Pharisees and Sadducees coming to where he was baptizing that they needed to do something to show they had really given up their _____. (2.1)

2. John baptized with water. How was Jesus going to baptize? With the _____ _____ and with fire. (2.1)

3. It is the _____ of God who takes away the sin of the world. (2.5)

4. Jesus' first miracle was turning the _____ into _____ . What was the result? "There Jesus showed His _____, and His disciples put their _____ in Him." (2.8)

5. Why didn't Jesus let them have power over him? He knew what was in their _____. (2.9)

6. What did Jesus tell Nicodemus is necessary in order to see the kingdom of God? "Don't be surprised when I say, 'You must be _____.'" (2.10)

7. God loved the people of this world so much that He gave His only Son, so that everyone who has faith in Him will have _____ _____. (2.10)

8. What did Jesus promise would happen to the woman at the well if she drank the water that He had to give? She would never be _____ again. (2.13)

9. What did many of the Samaritans end up saying about Jesus? "We have heard Him ourselves, and we are certain that He is the _____ of the _____." (2.15)

10. At first, the people in Jesus' hometown of Nazareth spoke well of Him and were amazed at the _____ things He said. But when He said to them what they did not want to hear, they dragged Him to the edge of the_____ on which the town was built, because they wanted to _____ Him down. (2.18)

11. When Jesus told the good news of God, He said, "God's kingdom will soon be here. _____ _____ to God and _____ the good news." (2.19)

3 The Year of Popularity

3.1 The Calling of the First Disciples

While Jesus was walking along the shore of Lake Galilee, he saw two brothers. One was Simon, also known as Peter, and the other was Andrew. They were fishermen, and they were casting their net into the lake. Jesus said to them, "Come with me! I will teach you how to bring in people instead of fish." Right then the two brothers dropped their nets and went with him.

Jesus walked on until he saw James and John, the sons of Zebedee. They were in a boat with their father, mending their nets. Jesus asked them to come with him too. Right away they left the boat and their father and went with Jesus. [23]

Jesus was standing on the shore of Lake Gennesaret, teaching the people as they crowded around him to hear God's message. Near the shore he saw two boats left there by some fishermen who had gone to wash their nets. Jesus got into the boat that belonged to Simon and asked him to row it out a little way from the shore. Then Jesus sat down in the boat to teach the crowd.

When Jesus had finished speaking, he told Simon, "Row the boat out into the deep water and let your nets down to catch some fish."

"Master," Simon answered, "we have worked hard all night long and have not caught a thing. But if you tell me to, I will let the nets down." They did it and caught so many fish that their nets began ripping apart. Then they signaled for their partners in the other boat to come and help them. The men came, and together they filled the two boats so full that they both began to sink.

When Simon Peter saw this happen, he knelt down in front of Jesus and said, "Lord, don't come near me! I am a sinner." Peter and everyone with him were completely surprised at all the fish they had caught. His partners James and John, the sons of Zebedee, were surprised too.

Jesus told Simon, "Don't be afraid! From now on you will bring in people instead of fish." The men pulled their boats up on the shore. Then they left everything and went with Jesus. [24]

3.2 Jesus Drives Out an Evil Spirit

Jesus and his disciples went to the town of Capernaum. Then on the next Sabbath he went into the Jewish meeting place and started teaching. Everyone was amazed at his teaching. He taught with authority, and not like the teachers of the Law of Moses. Suddenly a man with an evil spirit in him entered the meeting place and yelled, "Jesus from Nazareth, what do you want with us? Have you come to destroy us? I know who you are! You are God's Holy One."

Jesus told the evil spirit, "Be quiet and come out of the man!" The spirit shook him. Then it gave a loud shout and left.

Everyone was completely surprised and kept saying to each other, "What is this? It must be some new kind of powerful teaching! Even the evil spirits obey him." News about Jesus quickly spread all over Galilee.

3.3 Jesus Heals Many

As soon as Jesus left the meeting place with James and John, they went home with Simon and Andrew. When they got there, Jesus was told that Simon's mother-in-law was sick in bed with fever. Jesus went to her. He took hold of her hand and helped her up. The fever left her, and she served them a meal.

That evening after sunset, all who were sick or had demons in them were brought to Jesus. In fact, the whole town gathered around the door of the house. Jesus healed all kinds of terrible diseases and forced out a lot of demons. But the demons knew who he was, and he did not let them speak.

3.4 Jesus Prays in a Solitary Place

Very early the next morning, Jesus got up and went to a place where he could be alone and pray. Simon and the others started looking for him. And when they found him, they said, "Everyone is looking for you!"

Jesus replied, "We must go to the nearby towns, so that I can tell the good news to those people. This is why I have come." [25]

3.5 Jesus Heals the Sick

Jesus went all over Galilee, teaching in the Jewish meeting places and preaching the good news about God's kingdom. He also healed every kind of disease and sickness. News about him spread all over Syria, and people with every kind of sickness or disease were brought to him. Some of them had a lot of demons in them, others were thought to be crazy, and still others could not walk. But Jesus healed them all.

Large crowds followed Jesus from Galilee and the region around the ten cities known as Decapolis. They also came from Jerusalem, Judea, and from across the Jordan River. [26]

3.6 A Man With Leprosy

A man with leprosy came to Jesus and knelt down. He begged, "You have the power to make me well, if only you wanted to."

Jesus felt sorry for the man. So he put his hand on him and said, "I want to! Now you are well." At once the man's leprosy disappeared, and he was well.

After Jesus strictly warned the man, he sent him on his way. He said, "Don't tell anyone about this. Just go and show the priest that you are well. Then take a gift to the temple as Moses commanded, and everyone will know that you have been healed."

The man talked about it so much and told so many people, that Jesus could no longer go openly into a town. He had to stay away from the towns, but people still came to him from everywhere.

3.7 Jesus Heals a Crippled Man

Jesus went back to Capernaum, and a few days later people heard that he was at home. Then so many of them came to the house that there wasn't even standing room left in front of the door.

Jesus was still teaching when four people came up, carrying a crippled man on a mat. But because of the crowd, they could not get him to Jesus. So they made a hole in the roof above him and let the man down in front of everyone.

When Jesus saw how much faith they had, he said to the crippled man, "My friend, your sins are forgiven."

Some of the teachers of the Law of Moses were sitting there. They started wondering, "Why would he say such a thing? He must think he is God! Only God can forgive sins."

Right away, Jesus knew what they were thinking, and he said, "Why are you thinking such things? Is it easier for me to tell this crippled man that his sins are forgiven or to tell him to get up and pick up his mat and go on home? I will show you that the Son of Man has the right to forgive sins here on earth." So Jesus said to the man, "Get up! Pick up your mat and go on home."

The man got right up. He picked up his mat and went out while everyone watched in amazement. They praised God and said, "We have never seen anything like this!"

3.8 The Calling of Levi

Once again, Jesus went to the shore of Lake Galilee. A large crowd gathered around him, and he taught them. As he walked along, he saw Levi, the son of Alphaeus. Levi was sitting at the place for paying taxes, and Jesus said to him, "Come with me!" So he got up and went with Jesus.

Later, Jesus and his disciples were having dinner at Levi's house. Many tax collectors and other sinners had become followers of Jesus, and they were also guests at the dinner.

Some of the teachers of the Law of Moses were Pharisees, and they saw that Jesus was eating with sinners and tax collectors. So they asked his disciples, "Why does he eat with tax collectors and sinners?"

Jesus heard them and answered, "Healthy people don't need a doctor, but sick people do. I didn't come to invite good people to be my followers. I came to invite sinners." [27]

3.9 Jesus Questioned About Fasting

Some people said to Jesus, "John's followers often pray and go without eating, and so do the followers of the Pharisees. But your disciples never go without eating or drinking."

Jesus told them, "The friends of a bridegroom don't go without eating while he is still with them. But the time will come when he will be taken from them. Then they will go without eating."

Jesus then told them these sayings:

No one uses a new piece of cloth to patch old clothes. The patch would shrink and make the hole even bigger.

No one pours new wine into old wineskins. The new wine would swell and burst the old skins. Then the wine would be lost, and the skins would be ruined. New wine must be put only into new wineskins.

No one wants new wine after drinking old wine. They say, "The old wine is better." [28]

3.10 The Healing at the Pool

Later, Jesus went to Jerusalem for another Jewish festival. In the city near the sheep gate was a pool with five porches, and its name in Hebrew was Bethzatha.

Many sick, blind, lame, and crippled people were lying close to the pool.

Beside the pool was a man who had been sick for thirty-eight years. When Jesus saw the man and realized that he had been crippled for a long time, he asked him, "Do you want to be healed?"

The man answered, "Lord, I don't have anyone to put me in the pool when the water is stirred up. I try to get in, but someone else always gets there first."

Jesus told him, "Pick up your mat and walk!" Right then the man was healed. He picked up his mat and started walking around. The day on which this happened was a Sabbath.

When the Jewish leaders saw the man carrying his mat, they said to him, "This is the Sabbath! No one is allowed to carry a mat on the Sabbath."

But he replied, "The man who healed me told me to pick up my mat and walk."

They asked him, "Who is this man that told you to pick up your mat and walk?" But he did not know who Jesus was, and Jesus had left because of the crowd.

Later, Jesus met the man in the temple and told him, "You are now well. But don't sin anymore or something worse might happen to you." The man left and told the leaders that Jesus was the one who had healed him. They started making a lot of trouble for Jesus because he did things like this on the Sabbath.

But Jesus said, "My Father has never stopped working, and that is why I keep on working." Now the leaders wanted to kill Jesus for two reasons. First, he had broken the law of the Sabbath. But even worse, he had said that God was his Father, which made him equal with God.

3.11 Life Through the Son

Jesus told the people:

I tell you for certain that the Son cannot do anything on his own. He can do only what he sees the Father doing, and he does exactly what he sees the Father do. The Father loves the Son and has shown him everything he does. The Father will show him even greater things, and you will be amazed. Just as the Father raises the dead and gives life, so the Son gives life to anyone he wants to.

The Father doesn't judge anyone, but he has made his Son the judge of everyone. The Father wants all people to honor the Son as much as they honor him. When anyone refuses to honor the Son, that is the same as refusing to honor the Father who sent him. I tell you for certain that everyone who hears my message and has faith in the one who sent me has eternal life and will never be condemned. They have already gone from death to life.

I tell you for certain that the time will come, and it is already here, when all of the dead will hear the voice of the Son of God. And those who listen to it will live! The Father has the power to give life, and he has given that same power to the Son. And he has given his Son the right to judge everyone, because he is the Son of Man.

Don't be surprised! The time will come when all of the dead will hear the voice of the Son of Man, and they will come out of their graves. Everyone who has done good things will rise to life, but everyone who has done evil things will rise and be condemned.

I cannot do anything on my own. The Father sent me, and he is the one who told me how to judge. I judge with fairness, because I obey him, and I don't just try to please myself.

3.12 Testimonies About Jesus

If I speak for myself, there is no way to prove I am telling the truth. But there is someone else who speaks for me, and I know what he says is true. You sent messengers to John, and he told them the truth. I don't depend on what people say about me, but I tell you these things so that you may be saved. John was a lamp that gave a lot of light, and you were glad to enjoy his light for a while.

But something more important than John speaks for me. I mean the things that the Father has given me to do! All of these speak for me and prove that the Father sent me.

The Father who sent me also speaks for me, but you have never heard his voice or seen him face to face. You have not believed his message, because you refused to have faith in the one he sent.

You search the Scriptures, because you think you will find eternal life in them. The Scriptures tell about me, but you refuse to come to me for eternal life.

I don't care about human praise, but I do know that none of you love God. I have come with my Father's authority, and you have not welcomed me. But you will welcome people who come on their own. How could you possibly believe? You like to have your friends praise you, and you don't care about praise that the only God can give!

Don't think that I will be the one to accuse you to the

Father. You have put your hope in Moses, yet he is the very one who will accuse you. Moses wrote about me, and if you had believed Moses, you would have believed me. But if you don't believe what Moses wrote, how can you believe what I say?" [29]

3.13 Lord of the Sabbath

One Sabbath Jesus and his disciples were walking through some wheat fields. His disciples were picking grains of wheat as they went along. Some Pharisees asked Jesus, "Why are your disciples picking grain on the Sabbath? They are not supposed to do that!"

Jesus answered, "Haven't you read what David did when he and his followers were hungry and in need? It was during the time of Abiathar the high priest. David went into the house of God and ate the sacred loaves of bread that only priests are allowed to eat. He also gave some to his followers. [30]

Haven't you read in the Law of Moses that the priests are allowed to work in the temple on the Sabbath? But no one says that they are guilty of breaking the law of the Sabbath. I tell you that there is something here greater than the temple. Don't you know what the Scriptures mean when they say, "Instead of offering sacrifices to me, I want you to be merciful to others?" If you knew what this means, you would not condemn these innocent disciples of mine. [31]

Jesus finished by saying, "People were not made for the good of the Sabbath. The Sabbath was made for the good of people. So the Son of Man is Lord over the Sabbath." [32]

Jesus left and went into one of the Jewish meeting places, where there was a man whose hand was crippled. Some Pharisees wanted to accuse Jesus of doing something wrong, and they asked him, "Is it right to heal someone on the Sabbath?"

Jesus answered, "If you had a sheep that fell into a ditch on the Sabbath, wouldn't you lift it out? People are worth much more than sheep, and so it is right to do good on the Sabbath." Then Jesus told the man, "Hold out your hand." The man did, and it became as healthy as the other one.

The Pharisees left and started making plans to kill Jesus. [33]

3.14 Crowds Follow Jesus

Jesus led his disciples down to the shore of the lake. Large crowds followed him from Galilee, Judea, and Jerusalem. People came from Idumea, as well as other places east of the Jordan River. They also came from the region around the cities of Tyre and Sidon. All of these crowds came because they had heard what Jesus was doing. He even had to tell his disciples to get a boat ready to keep him from being crushed by the crowds.

After Jesus had healed many people, the other sick people begged him to let them touch him. And whenever any evil spirits saw Jesus, they would fall to the ground and shout, "You are the Son of God!" But Jesus warned the spirits not to tell who he was.[34]

So God's promise came true, just as Isaiah the prophet had said,

"Here is my chosen servant!
  I love him, and he pleases me.
I will give him my Spirit,
  and he will bring justice to the nations.
He won't shout or yell
  or call out in the streets.
He won't break off a bent reed
or put out a dying flame,
  but he will make sure that justice is done.
 All nations will place their hope in him." [35]

Jesus and his apostles went down from the mountain and came to some flat, level ground. Many other disciples were there to meet him. Large crowds of people from all over Judea, Jerusalem, and the coastal cities of Tyre and Sidon were there too. These people had come to listen to Jesus and to be healed of their diseases. All who were troubled by evil spirits were also healed. Everyone was trying to touch Jesus, because power was going out from him and healing them all.[36]

3.15 The Appointing of the Twelve Apostles

About that time Jesus went off to a mountain to pray, and he spent the whole night there. The next morning he called his disciples together and chose twelve of them to be his apostles, [37] so that they could be with him. He also wanted to send them out to preach and to force out demons. Simon was one of the twelve, and Jesus named him Peter. There were also James and John, the two sons of Zebedee. Jesus called them Boanerges, which means "Thunderbolts." Andrew, Philip, Bartholomew, Matthew, Thomas, James son of Alphaeus, and Thaddaeus were also apostles. The others were Simon, known as the Eager One, and Judas Iscariot, who later betrayed Jesus.[38]

The Sermon on the Mount (3.16-34)

3.16 The Beatitudes

When Jesus saw the crowds, he went up on the side of a mountain and sat down. Jesus' disciples gathered around him, and he taught them:

God blesses those people who depend only on him.
 They belong to the kingdom of heaven!
God blesses those people who grieve.
 They will find comfort!
God blesses those people who are humble.
 The earth will belong to them!
God blesses those people who want to obey him
more than to eat or drink.
 They will be given what they want!
God blesses those people who are merciful.
 They will be treated with mercy!
God blesses those people whose hearts are pure.
 They will see him!
God blesses those people who make peace.
 They will be called his children!
God blesses those people
who are treated badly for doing right.
 They belong to the kingdom of heaven!

God will bless you when people insult you, mistreat you, and tell all kinds of evil lies about you because of me. Be happy and excited! You will have a great reward in heaven. People did these same things to the prophets who lived long ago.

3.17 Salt and Light

You are like salt for everyone on earth. But if salt no longer tastes like salt, how can it make food salty? All it is good for is to be thrown out and walked on.

You are like light for the whole world. A city built on top of a hill cannot be hidden, and no one would light a lamp and put it under a clay pot. A lamp is placed on a lampstand, where it can give light to everyone in the house. Make your light shine, so that others will see the good that you do and will praise your Father in heaven.

3.18 The Fulfillment of the Law

Don't suppose that I came to do away with the Law and the Prophets. I did not come to do away with them, but to give them their full meaning. Heaven and earth may disappear. But I promise you that not even a period or comma will ever disappear from the Law. Everything written in it must happen.

If you reject even the least important command in the Law and teach others to do the same, you will be the least important person in the kingdom of heaven. But if you obey and teach others its commands, you will have an important place in the kingdom. You must obey God's commands better than the Pharisees and the teachers of the Law obey them. If you don't, I promise you that you will never get into the kingdom of heaven.

3.19 Murder

You know that our ancestors were told, "Do not murder" and "A murderer must be brought to trial." But I promise you that if you are angry with someone, you will have to stand trial. If you call someone a fool, you will be taken to court. And if you say that someone is worthless, you will be in danger of the fires of hell.

So if you are about to place your gift on the altar and remember that someone is angry with you, leave your gift there in front of the altar. Make peace with that person, then come back and offer your gift to God.

Before you are dragged into court, make friends with the person who has accused you of doing wrong. If you don't, you will be handed over to the judge and then to the officer who will put you in jail. I promise you that you will not get out until you have paid the last cent you owe.

3.20 Adultery

You know the commandment which says, "Be faithful in marriage." But I tell you that if you look at another woman and want her, you are already unfaithful in your thoughts. If your right eye causes you to sin, poke it out and throw it away. It is better to lose one part of your body, than for your whole body to end up in hell. If your right hand causes you to sin, chop it off and throw it away! It is better to lose one part of your body, than for your whole body to be thrown into hell.

Mercy Arce

478-6442 Am

9836 Palazzo Dr.
Stockton, CA.

we meet last
Sat. of month
1 p.m — 5 or 6 p.m

3.21 Divorce

You have been taught that a man who divorces his wife must write out divorce papers for her. But I tell you not to divorce your wife unless she has committed some terrible sexual sin. If you divorce her, you will cause her to be unfaithful, just as any man who marries her is guilty of taking another man's wife.

3.22 Oaths

You know that our ancestors were told, "Don't use the Lord's name to make a promise unless you are going to keep it." But I tell you not to swear by anything when you make a promise! Heaven is God's throne, so don't swear by heaven. The earth is God's footstool, so don't swear by the earth. Jerusalem is the city of the great king, so don't swear by it. Don't swear by your own head. You cannot make one hair white or black. When you make a promise, say only "Yes" or "No." Anything else comes from the devil.

3.23 An Eye for an Eye

You know that you have been taught, "An eye for an eye and a tooth for a tooth." But I tell you not to try to get even with a person who has done something to you. When someone slaps your right cheek, turn and let that person slap your other cheek. If someone sues you for your shirt, give up your coat as well. If a soldier forces you to carry his pack one mile, carry it two miles. When people ask you for something, give it to them. When they want to borrow money, lend it to them.

3.24 Love for Enemies

You have heard people say, "Love your neighbors and hate your enemies." But I tell you to love your enemies and pray for anyone who mistreats you. Then you will be acting like your Father in heaven. He makes the sun rise on both good and bad people. And he sends rain for the ones who do right and for the ones who do wrong. If you love only those people who love you, will God reward you for that? Even tax collectors love their friends. If you greet only your friends, what's so great about that? Don't even unbelievers do that? But you must always act like your Father in heaven.

3.25 Giving to the Poor

When you do good deeds, don't try to show off. If you do, you won't get a reward from your Father in heaven.

When you give to the poor, don't blow a loud horn. That's what show-offs do in the meeting places and on the street corners, because they are always looking for praise. I can assure you that they already have their reward.

When you give to the poor, don't let anyone know about it. Then your gift will be given in secret. Your Father knows what is done in secret, and he will reward you.

3.26 Prayer

When you pray, don't be like those show-offs who love to stand up and pray in the meeting places and on the street corners. They do this just to look good. I can assure you that they already have their reward.

When you pray, go into a room alone and close the door. Pray to your Father in private. He knows what is done in private, and he will reward you.

When you pray, don't talk on and on as people do who don't know God. They think God likes to hear long prayers. Don't be like them. Your Father knows what you need before you ask.

You should pray like this:

Our Father in heaven,
>   help us to honor your name.
Come and set up your kingdom,
>   so that everyone on earth will obey you,
>   as you are obeyed in heaven.
Give us our food for today.
Forgive us for doing wrong,
>   as we forgive others.
Keep us from being tempted
>   and protect us from evil.

If you forgive others for the wrongs they do to you, your Father in heaven will forgive you. But if you don't forgive others, your Father will not forgive your sins.

3.27 Fasting

When you go without eating, don't try to look gloomy as those show-offs do when they go without eating. I can assure you that they already have their reward. Instead, comb your hair and wash your face. Then others won't know that you are going without eating. But your Father sees what is done in private, and he will reward you.

3.28 Treasures in Heaven

Don't store up treasures on earth! Moths and rust can destroy them, and thieves can break in and steal them. Instead, store up your treasures in heaven, where moths and rust cannot destroy them, and thieves cannot break in and steal them. Your heart will always be where your treasure is.

Your eyes are like a window for your body. When they are good, you have all the light you need. But when your eyes are bad, everything is dark. If the light inside you is dark, you surely are in the dark.

You cannot be the slave of two masters! You will like one more than the other or be more loyal to one than the other. You cannot serve both God and money.

3.29 Do Not Worry

I tell you not to worry about your life. Don't worry about having something to eat, drink, or wear. Isn't life more than food or clothing? Look at the birds in the sky! They don't plant or harvest. They don't even store grain in barns. Yet your Father in heaven takes care of them. Aren't you worth more than birds?

Can worry make you live longer? Why worry about clothes? Look how the wild flowers grow. They don't work hard to make their clothes. But I tell you that Solomon with all his wealth wasn't as well clothed as one of them. God gives such beauty to everything that grows in the fields, even though it is here today and thrown into a fire tomorrow. He will surely do even more for you! Why do you have such little faith?

Don't worry and ask yourselves, "Will we have anything to eat? Will we have anything to drink? Will we have any clothes to wear?" Only people who don't know God are always worrying about such things. Your Father in heaven knows that you need all of these. But more than anything else, put God's work first and do what he wants. Then the other things will be yours as well.

Don't worry about tomorrow. It will take care of itself. You have enough to worry about today.

3.30 Condemning Others

Don't condemn others, and God won't condemn you. God will be as hard on you as you are on others! He will treat you exactly as you treat them.

You can see the speck in your friend's eye, but you don't notice the log in your own eye. How can you say, "My friend, let me take the speck out of your eye," when you don't see the log in your own eye? You're nothing but show-offs! First, take the log out of your own eye. Then you can see how to take the speck out of your friend's eye.

Don't give to dogs what belongs to God. They will only turn and attack you. Don't throw pearls down in front of pigs. They will trample all over them.

3.31 Ask, Search, Knock

Ask, and you will receive. Search, and you will find. Knock, and the door will be opened for you. Everyone who asks will receive. Everyone who searches will find. And the door will be opened for everyone who knocks. Would any of you give your hungry child a stone, if the child asked for some bread? Would you give your child a snake if the child asked for a fish? As bad as you are, you still know how to give good gifts to your children. But your heavenly Father is even more ready to give good things to people who ask.

Treat others as you want them to treat you. This is what the Law and the Prophets are all about.

3.32 The Narrow and Wide Gates

Go in through the narrow gate. The gate to destruction is wide, and the road that leads there is easy to follow. A lot of people go through that gate. But the gate to life is very narrow. The road that leads there is so hard to follow that only a few people find it.

3.33 A Tree and Its Fruit

Watch out for false prophets! They dress up like sheep, but inside they are wolves who have come to attack you. You can tell what they are by what they do. No one picks grapes or figs from thornbushes. A good tree produces good fruit, and a bad tree produces bad fruit. A good tree cannot produce bad fruit, and a bad tree cannot produce good fruit. Every tree that produces bad fruit will be chopped down and burned. You can tell who the false prophets are by their deeds.

Not everyone who calls me their Lord will get into the kingdom of heaven. Only the ones who obey my Father in heaven will get in. On the day of judgment many will call me their Lord. They will say, "We preached in your name, and in your name we forced out demons and worked many miracles." But I will tell them, "I will have nothing to do with you! Get out of my sight, you evil people! "

3.34 The Wise and Foolish Builders

Anyone who hears and obeys these teachings of mine is like a wise person who built a house on solid rock. Rain poured down, rivers flooded, and winds beat against that house. But it did not fall, because it was built on solid rock.

Anyone who hears my teachings and doesn't obey them is like a foolish person who built a house on sand. The rain poured down, the rivers flooded, and the winds blew and beat against that house. Finally, it fell with a crash.

When Jesus finished speaking, the crowds were surprised at his teaching. He taught them like someone with authority, and not like their teachers of the Law of Moses.

As Jesus came down the mountain, he was followed by large crowds.[39]

3.35 The Faith of the Army Officer

When Jesus was going into the town of Capernaum, an army officer came up to him and said, "Lord, my servant is at home in such terrible pain that he can't even move."

"I will go and heal him," Jesus replied.

But the officer said, "Lord, I'm not good enough for you to come into my house. Just give the order, and my servant will get well. I have officers who give orders to me, and I have soldiers who take orders from me. I can say to one of them, 'Go!' and he goes. I can say to another, 'Come!' and he comes. I can say to my servant, 'Do this!' and he will do it."

When Jesus heard this, he was so surprised that he turned and said to the crowd following him, "I tell you that in all of Israel I've never found anyone with this much faith! Many people will come from everywhere to enjoy the feast in the kingdom of heaven with Abraham, Isaac, and Jacob. But the ones who should have been in the kingdom will be thrown out into the dark. They will cry and grit their teeth in pain."

Then Jesus said to the officer, "You may go home now. Your faith has made it happen."

Right then his servant was healed.[40]

3.36 Jesus Raises a Widow's Son

Soon Jesus and his disciples were on their way to the town of Nain, and a big crowd was going along with them. As they came near the gate of the town, they saw people carrying out the body of a widow's only son. Many people from the town were walking along with her.

When the Lord saw the woman, he felt sorry for her and said, "Don't cry!"

Jesus went over and touched the stretcher on which the people were carrying the dead boy. They stopped, and Jesus said, "Young man, get up!" The boy sat up and began to speak. Jesus then gave him back to his mother.

Everyone was frightened and praised God. They said, "A great prophet is here with us! God has come to his people."

News about Jesus spread all over Judea and everywhere else in that part of the country.

3.37 Jesus and John the Baptist

John's followers told John everything that was being said about Jesus. So he sent two of them to ask the Lord, "Are you the one we should be looking for? Or must we wait for someone else?"

When these messengers came to Jesus, they said, "John the Baptist sent us to ask, 'Are you the one we should be looking for? Or are we supposed to wait for someone else?'"

At that time Jesus was healing many people who were sick or in pain or were troubled by evil spirits, and he was giving sight to a lot of blind people. Jesus said to the messengers sent by John, "Go and tell John what you have seen and heard. Blind people are now able to see, and the lame can walk. People who have leprosy are being healed, and the deaf can now hear. The dead are raised to life, and the poor are hearing the good news. God will bless everyone who doesn't reject me because of what I do."

After John's messengers had gone, Jesus began speaking to the crowds about John:

> What kind of person did you go out to the desert to see? Was he like tall grass blown about by the wind? What kind of man did you really go out to see? Was he someone dressed in fine clothes? People who wear expensive clothes and live in luxury are in the king's palace. What then did you go out to see? Was he a prophet? He certainly was! I tell you that he was more than a prophet. In the Scriptures, God calls John his messenger and says, "I am sending my messenger ahead of you to get things ready for you." No one ever born on this earth is greater than John. But whoever is least important in God's kingdom is greater than John.

Everyone had been listening to John. Even the tax collectors had obeyed God and had done what was right by letting John baptize them. But the Pharisees and the experts in the Law of Moses refused to obey God and be baptized by John.

Jesus went on to say:

What are you people like? What kind of people are you? You are like children sitting in the market and shouting to each other,
"We played the flute,
    but you would not dance!
We sang a funeral song,
    but you would not cry!"
John the Baptist did not go around eating and drinking, and you said, "John has a demon in him!" But because the Son of Man goes around eating and drinking, you say, "Jesus eats and drinks too much! He is even a friend of tax collectors and sinners." Yet Wisdom is shown to be right by what its followers do.[41]

3.38 Rest for the Tired

At that moment Jesus said:
My Father, Lord of heaven and earth, I am grateful that you hid all this from wise and educated people and showed it to ordinary people. Yes, Father, that is what pleased you.

My Father has given me everything, and he is the only one who knows the Son. The only one who truly knows the Father is the Son. But the Son wants to tell others about the Father, so that they can know him too.

If you are tired from carrying heavy burdens, come to me and I will give you rest. Take the yoke I give you. Put it on your shoulders and learn from me. I am gentle and humble, and you will find rest. This yoke is easy to bear, and this burden is light.[42]

3.39 Jesus Anointed by a Sinful Woman

A Pharisee invited Jesus to have dinner with him. So Jesus went to the Pharisee's home and got ready to eat.

When a sinful woman in that town found out that Jesus was there, she bought an expensive bottle of perfume. Then she came and stood behind Jesus. She cried and started washing his feet with her tears and drying them with her hair. The woman kissed his feet and poured the perfume on them.

The Pharisee who had invited Jesus saw this and said to himself, "If this man really were a prophet, he would know what kind of woman is touching him! He would know that she is a sinner."

Jesus said to the Pharisee, "Simon, I have something to say to you."
"Teacher, what is it?" Simon replied.
Jesus told him, "Two people were in debt to a moneylender. One of

them owed him five hundred silver coins, and the other owed him fifty. Since neither of them could pay him back, the moneylender said that they didn't have to pay him anything. Which one of them will like him more?"

Simon answered, "I suppose it would be the one who had owed more and didn't have to pay it back."

"You are right," Jesus said.

He turned toward the woman and said to Simon, "Have you noticed this woman? When I came into your home, you didn't give me any water so I could wash my feet. But she has washed my feet with her tears and dried them with her hair. You didn't greet me with a kiss, but from the time I came in, she has not stopped kissing my feet. You didn't even pour olive oil on my head, but she has poured expensive perfume on my feet. So I tell you that all her sins are forgiven, and that is why she has shown great love. But anyone who has been forgiven for only a little will show only a little love."

Then Jesus said to the woman, "Your sins are forgiven."

Some other guests started saying to one another, "Who is this who dares to forgive sins?"

But Jesus told the woman, "Because of your faith, you are now saved. May God give you peace!"

3.40 Jesus in Galilee

Soon after this, Jesus was going through towns and villages, telling the good news about God's kingdom. His twelve apostles were with him, and so were some women who had been healed of evil spirits and all sorts of diseases. One of the women was Mary Magdalene, who once had seven demons in her. Joanna, Susanna, and many others had also used what they owned to help Jesus and his disciples. Joanna's husband Chuza was one of Herod's officials. [43]

3.41 Jesus and Beelzebul

Some people brought to Jesus a man who was blind and could not talk because he had a demon in him. Jesus healed the man, and then he was able to talk and see. The crowds were so amazed that they asked, "Could Jesus be the Son of David?"

When the Pharisees heard this, they said, "He forces out demons by the power of Beelzebul, the ruler of the demons!"

Jesus knew what they were thinking, and he said to them:

Any kingdom where people fight each other will end up ruined. And a town or family that fights will soon destroy itself. So if Satan fights against himself, how can his kingdom last? If I use the power of Beelzebul to force out demons, whose power do your own followers use to force them out? Your followers are the ones who will judge you. But when I force out demons by the power of God's Spirit, it proves that God's kingdom has already come to you. How can anyone break into a strong man's house and steal his things, unless he first ties up the strong man? Then he can take everything.

If you are not on my side, you are against me. If you don't gather in the harvest with me, you scatter it. I tell you that any sinful thing you do or say can be forgiven. Even if you speak against the Son of Man, you can be forgiven. But if you speak against the Holy Spirit, you can never be forgiven, either in this life or in the life to come.

A good tree produces only good fruit, and a bad tree produces bad fruit. You can tell what a tree is like by the fruit it produces. You are a bunch of evil snakes, so how can you say anything good? Your words show what is in your hearts. Good people bring good things out of their hearts, but evil people bring evil things out of their hearts. I promise you that on the day of judgment, everyone will have to account for every careless word they have spoken. On that day they will be told that they are either innocent or guilty because of the things they have said.

3.42 The Sign of Jonah

Some Pharisees and teachers of the Law of Moses said, "Teacher, we want you to show us a sign from heaven."

But Jesus replied:

You want a sign because you are evil and won't believe! But the only sign you will get is the sign of the prophet Jonah. He was in the stomach of a big fish for three days and nights, just as the Son of Man will be deep in the earth for three days and nights. On the day of judgment the people of Nineveh will stand there with you and condemn you. They turned to God when Jonah preached, and yet here is something far greater than Jonah. The Queen of the South will also stand there with you and condemn you. She traveled a long way to hear Solomon's wisdom, and yet here is something much greater than Solomon.

When an evil spirit leaves a person, it travels through the desert, looking for a place to rest. But when the demon doesn't find a place, it says, "I will go back to the home I left." When it gets there and finds the place empty, clean, and fixed up, it goes off and finds seven other evil spirits even worse than itself. They all come and make their home there, and the person ends up in worse shape than before. That's how it will be with you evil people of today.

3.43 Jesus' Mother and Brothers

While Jesus was still speaking to the crowds, his mother and brothers came and stood outside because they wanted to talk with him. Someone told Jesus, "Your mother and brothers are standing outside and want to talk with you."

Jesus answered, "Who is my mother and who are my brothers?" Then he pointed to his disciples and said, "These are my mother and my brothers! Anyone who obeys my Father in heaven is my brother or sister or mother." 44

While Jesus was still talking, a woman in the crowd spoke up, "The woman who gave birth to you and nursed you is blessed!"

Jesus replied, "That's true, but the people who are really blessed are the ones who hear and obey God's message!" 45

3.44 The Parable of the Farmer

That same day Jesus left the house and went out beside Lake Galilee, where he sat down to teach. Such large crowds gathered around him that he had to sit in a boat, while the people stood on the shore. Then he taught them many things by using stories. He said:

> A farmer went out to scatter seed in a field. While the farmer was scattering the seed, some of it fell along the road and was eaten by birds. Other seeds fell on thin, rocky ground and quickly started growing because the soil wasn't very deep. But when the sun came up, the plants were scorched and dried up, because they did not have enough roots. Some other seeds fell where thornbushes grew up and choked the plants. But a few seeds did fall on good ground where the plants produced a hundred or sixty or thirty times as much as was scattered. If you have ears, pay attention!

Jesus' disciples came to him and asked, "Why do you use nothing but stories when you speak to the people?"

Jesus answered:

> I have explained the secrets about the kingdom of heaven to you, but not to others. Everyone who has something will be given more. But people who don't have anything will lose even what little they have. I use stories when I speak to them because when they look, they cannot see, and when they listen, they cannot hear or

understand. So God's promise came true, just as the prophet Isaiah had said,

"These people will listen and listen,
　but never understand.
They will look and look, but never see.
　All of them have stubborn minds!
Their ears are stopped up, and their eyes are covered.
　They cannot see or hear or understand.
If they could, they would turn to me,
and I would heal them."

　　But God has blessed you, because your eyes can see and your ears can hear! Many prophets and good people were eager to see what you see and to hear what you hear. But I tell you that they did not see or hear.
Now listen to the meaning of the story about the farmer:
　　The seeds that fell along the road are the people who hear the message about the kingdom, but don't understand it. Then the evil one comes and snatches the message from their hearts. The seeds that fell on rocky ground are the people who gladly hear the message and accept it right away. But they don't have deep roots, and they don't last very long. As soon as life gets hard or the message gets them in trouble, they give up.
　　The seeds that fell among the thornbushes are also people who hear the message. But they start worrying about the needs of this life and are fooled by the desire to get rich. So the message gets choked out, and they never produce anything. The seeds that fell on good ground are the people who hear and understand the message. They produce as much as a hundred or sixty or thirty times what was planted. [46]

3.45　A Lamp on a Stand

Jesus also said:
　　You don't light a lamp and put it under a clay pot or under a bed. Don't you put a lamp on a lampstand? There is nothing hidden that will not be made public. There is no secret that will not be well known. If you have ears, pay attention!
　　Listen carefully to what you hear! The way you treat others will be the way you will be treated — and even worse. Everyone who has something will be given more. But people who don't have anything will lose what little they have.

3.46 The Parable of the Growing Seed

Again Jesus said:

God's kingdom is like what happens when a farmer scatters seed in a field. The farmer sleeps at night and is up and around during the day. Yet the seeds keep sprouting and growing, and he doesn't understand how. It is the ground that makes the seeds sprout and grow into plants that produce grain. Then when harvest season comes and the grain is ripe, the farmer cuts it with a sickle. [47]

3.47 The Parable of the Weeds

Jesus then told them this story:

The kingdom of heaven is like what happened when a farmer scattered good seed in a field. But while everyone was sleeping, an enemy came and scattered weed seeds in the field and then left.

When the plants came up and began to ripen, the farmer's servants could see the weeds. The servants came and asked, "Sir, didn't you scatter good seed in your field? Where did these weeds come from?"

"An enemy did this," he replied.

His servants then asked, "Do you want us to go out and pull up the weeds?"

"No!" he answered. "You might also pull up the wheat. Leave the weeds alone until harvest time. Then I'll tell my workers to gather the weeds and tie them up and burn them. But I'll have them store the wheat in my barn."

3.48 The Parables of the Mustard Seed and the Yeast

Jesus told them another story:

The kingdom of heaven is like what happens when a farmer plants a mustard seed in a field. Although it is the smallest of all seeds, it grows larger than any garden plant and becomes a tree. Birds even come and nest on its branches.

Jesus also said:

The kingdom of heaven is like what happens when a woman mixes a little yeast into three big batches of flour. Finally, all the dough rises. [48]

Jesus used many other stories when he spoke to the people, and he taught them as much as they could understand. He did not tell them anything without using stories. But when he was alone with his disciples, he explained everything to them. [49]

So God's promise came true, just as the prophet had said,

"I will use stories to speak my message
  and to explain things that have been hidden
  since the creation of the world."

3.49 The Parable of the Weeds Explained

After Jesus left the crowd and went inside, his disciples came to him and said, "Explain to us the story about the weeds in the wheat field." Jesus answered:

The one who scattered the good seed is the Son of Man. The field is the world, and the good seeds are the people who belong to the kingdom. The weed seeds are those who belong to the evil one, and the one who scattered them is the devil. The harvest is the end of time, and angels are the ones who bring in the harvest.

Weeds are gathered and burned. That's how it will be at the end of time. The Son of Man will send out his angels, and they will gather from his kingdom everyone who does wrong or causes others to sin. Then he will throw them into a flaming furnace, where people will cry and grit their teeth in pain. But everyone who has done right will shine like the sun in their Father's kingdom. If you have ears, pay attention!

3.50 The Parables of the Hidden Treasure and the Pearl

The kingdom of heaven is like what happens when someone finds treasure hidden in a field and buries it again. A person like that is happy and goes and sells everything in order to buy that field.

The kingdom of heaven is like what happens when a shop owner is looking for fine pearls. After finding a very valuable one, the owner goes and sells everything in order to buy that pearl.

3.51 The Parable of the Net

The kingdom of heaven is like what happens when a net is thrown into a lake and catches all kinds of fish. When the net is full, it is dragged to the shore, and the fishermen sit down to separate the fish. They keep the good ones, but throw the bad ones away. That's how it will be at the end of time. Angels will come and separate the evil people from the ones who have done right. Then those evil people will be thrown into a flaming furnace, where they will cry and grit their teeth in pain.

Jesus asked his disciples if they understood all these things. They said, "Yes, we do."

So he told them, "Every student of the Scriptures who becomes a disciple in the kingdom of heaven is like someone who brings out new and old treasures from the storeroom."

When Jesus had finished telling these stories, he left. [50]

3.52 Jesus Calms the Storm

That evening, Jesus said to his disciples, "Let's cross to the east side." So they left the crowd, and his disciples started across the lake with him in the boat. Some other boats followed along. Suddenly a windstorm struck the lake. Waves started splashing into the boat, and it was about to sink.

Jesus was in the back of the boat with his head on a pillow, and he was asleep. His disciples woke him and said, "Teacher, don't you care that we're about to drown?"

Jesus got up and ordered the wind and the waves to be quiet. The wind stopped, and everything was calm.

Jesus asked his disciples, "Why were you afraid? Don't you have any faith?"

Now they were more afraid than ever and said to each other, "Who is this? Even the wind and the waves obey him!" [51]

3.53 The Healing of a Demon-Possessed Man

Jesus and his disciples sailed across Lake Galilee and came to shore near the town of Gerasa. As Jesus was getting out of the boat, he was met by a man from that town. The man had demons in him. He had gone naked for a long time and no longer lived in a house, but in the graveyard. [52]

No one was able to tie the man up anymore, not even with a chain. He had often been put in chains and leg irons, but he broke the chains and smashed the leg irons. No one could control him. Night and day he was in the graveyard or on the hills, yelling and cutting himself with stones.

When the man saw Jesus in the distance, he ran up to him and knelt down. He shouted, "Jesus, Son of God in heaven, what do you want with me? Promise me in God's name that you won't torture me!" The man said this because Jesus had already told the evil spirit to come out of him.

Jesus asked, "What is your name?"

The man answered, "My name is Lots, because I have 'lots' of evil spirits." He then begged Jesus not to send them away.

Over on the hillside a large herd of pigs was feeding. So the evil spirits begged Jesus, "Send us into those pigs! Let us go into them." Jesus let them go, and they went out of the man and into the pigs. The whole herd of about two thousand pigs rushed down the steep bank into the lake and drowned.

The men taking care of the pigs ran to the town and the farms to spread the news. Then the people came out to see what had happened. When they came to Jesus, they saw the man who had once been full of demons. He was sitting there with his clothes on and in his right mind, and they were terrified.

Everyone who had seen what had happened told about the man and the pigs. Then the people started begging Jesus to leave their part of the country.

When Jesus was getting into the boat, the man begged to go with him. But Jesus would not let him. Instead, he said, "Go home to your family and tell them how much the Lord has done for you and how good he has been to you."

The man went away into the region near the ten cities known as Decapolis and began telling everyone how much Jesus had done for him. Everyone who heard what had happened was amazed.

3.54 A Dead Girl and a Sick Woman

Once again Jesus got into the boat and crossed Lake Galilee. Then as he stood on the shore, a large crowd gathered around him. The person in charge of the Jewish meeting place was also there. His name was Jairus, and when he saw Jesus, he went over to him. He knelt at Jesus' feet and started begging him for help. He said, "My daughter is about to die! Please come and touch her, so she will get well and live." Jesus went with Jairus. Many people followed along and kept crowding around.

In the crowd was a woman who had been bleeding for twelve years. She had gone to many doctors, and they had not done anything except cause her a lot of pain. She had paid them all the money she had. But instead of getting better, she only got worse.

The woman had heard about Jesus, so she came up behind him in the crowd and barely touched his clothes. She had said to herself, "If I can just touch his clothes, I will get well." As soon as she touched them, her bleeding stopped, and she knew she was well.

At that moment Jesus felt power go out from him. He turned to the crowd and asked, "Who touched my clothes?"

His disciples said to him, "Look at all these people crowding around you! How can you ask who touched you?" But Jesus turned to see who had touched him.

The woman knew what had happened to her. She came shaking with fear and knelt down in front of Jesus. Then she told him the whole story.

Jesus said to the woman, "You are now well because of your faith. May God give you peace! You are healed, and you will no longer be in pain."

While Jesus was still speaking, some men came from Jairus' home and said, "Your daughter has died! Why bother the teacher anymore?"

Jesus heard what they said, and he said to Jairus, "Don't worry. Just have faith!"

Jesus did not let anyone go with him except Peter and the two brothers, James and John. They went home with Jairus and saw the people crying and making a lot of noise. Then Jesus went inside and said to them, "Why are you crying and carrying on like this? The child isn't dead. She is just asleep." But the people laughed at him.

After Jesus had sent them all out of the house, he took the girl's father and mother and his three disciples and went to where she was. He took the twelve-year-old girl by the hand and said, "Talitha, koum!" which means, "Little girl, get up!" The girl got right up and started walking around.

Everyone was greatly surprised. But Jesus ordered them not to tell anyone what had happened. Then he said, "Give her something to eat." [53]

3.55 Jesus Heals the Blind and Mute

As Jesus was walking along, two blind men began following him and shouting, "Son of David, have pity on us!"

After Jesus had gone indoors, the two blind men came up to him. He asked them, "Do you believe I can make you well?"

"Yes, Lord," they answered.

Jesus touched their eyes and said, "Because of your faith, you will be healed." They were able to see, and Jesus strictly warned them not to tell anyone about him. But they left and talked about him to everyone in that part of the country.

As Jesus and his disciples were on their way, some people brought to him a man who could not talk because a demon was in him. After Jesus had forced the demon out, the man started talking. The crowds were so amazed that they began saying, "Nothing like this has ever happened in Israel!"

But the Pharisees said, "The leader of the demons gives him the power to force out demons." [54]

3.56 Jesus Rejected Again in His Hometown

Jesus left and returned to his hometown with his disciples. The next Sabbath he taught in the Jewish meeting place. Many of the people who heard him were amazed and asked, "How can he do all this? Where did he get such wisdom and the power to work these miracles? Isn't he the carpenter, the son of Mary? Aren't James, Joseph, Judas, and Simon his brothers? Don't his sisters still live here in our town?" The people were very unhappy because of what he was doing.

But Jesus said, "Prophets are honored by everyone, except the people of their hometown and their relatives and their own family." Jesus could not work any miracles there, except to heal a few sick people by placing his hands on them. He was surprised that the people did not have any faith. [55]

> The Pueblo have no word that translates as "religion." The knowledge of a spiritual life is a part of the person 24 hours a day, every day of the year. Religious beliefs permeates every aspect of life: it determines man's relation with the natural world and with his fellow man.
>
> **Joe S. Sando**
> **Jemez Pueblo**

REVIEW QUESTIONS, SECTION 3

1. When Jesus called to some fishermen, He said, "Come with me! I will _____ you how to bring in _____ instead of _____." (3.1)

2. The people at the Jewish meeting place in Capernaum were amazed at Jesus' teaching, because He taught them as one who had _____. (3.2)

3. Jesus saw the man with leprosy and put His _____ on him and made him _____. (3.6)

4. Jesus forgave the sins of the crippled man before healing him. If only God can forgive sins, what does this tell us about Jesus? That He is _____. (3.7)

5. Jesus said, "I didn't come to invite _____ _____ to be My followers, I came to invite _____." (3.8)

6. Why were the Jewish leaders trying so hard to kill Jesus? He said God was his Father, which made Him _____ with God. (3.10)

7. Who made plans to kill Jesus? The _____. (3.13)

8. The prophet _____ had said of God's chosen servant. "All nations will place their hope in Him." (3.14)

9. Jesus chose twelve to be His _____ so they could be with Him and that He might send them out to _____. (3.15)

10. Why do the show-offs pray? To look _____. (3.26)

11. We should put God's _____ first and do what He _____. (3.29)

12. The army officer accepted Jesus' authority. That was why Jesus told the people that He had not found anyone in Israel with this much _____. (3.35)

13. Jesus invited all who were tired from carrying heavy burdens to come to Him in order to find _____ .(3.38)

14. Jesus told Simon the Pharisee that the many sins of the sinful woman had been forgiven. Jesus told the woman her _____ had saved her. (3.39)

15. As Jesus was going from one town and village to another, He told the_____ _____ of the kingdom of God. (3.40)

16. Jesus taught that words show what is in your heart. We will be _____ or _____ by the things we have said. (3.41)

17. Jesus made it clear that His true family is made up of those who _____ the Father in heaven. (3.43)

18. In the story about the farmer, Jesus said the seeds that fell on good ground are the people who _____ and _____ the message. (3.44)

19. What did Jesus' disciples lack that made them afraid? They still had no _____. (3.52)

20. What did Jesus say healed the woman who had been subject to bleeding? "You are now well because of your _____." (3.54)

21. The two blind men were healed because of their _____. (3.55)

22. Jesus could not do any miracles in His hometown, except heal a few sick people. He was surprised that the people did not have any _____. (3.56)

4 The Year of Opposition

4.1 The Workers Are Few

Jesus went to every town and village. He taught in their meeting places and preached the good news about God's kingdom. Jesus also healed every kind of disease and sickness. When he saw the crowds, he felt sorry for them. They were confused and helpless, like sheep without a shepherd. He said to his disciples, "A large crop is in the fields, but there are only a few workers. Ask the Lord in charge of the harvest to send out workers to bring it in."

4.2 Jesus Sends Out the Twelve

Jesus called together his twelve disciples. He gave them the power to force out evil spirits and to heal every kind of disease and sickness. [56]
Jesus sent out the twelve apostles with these instructions:

Stay away from the Gentiles and don't go to any Samaritan town. Go only to the people of Israel, because they are like a flock of lost sheep. As you go, announce that the kingdom of heaven will soon be here. Heal the sick, raise the dead to life, heal people who have leprosy, and force out demons. You received without paying, now give without being paid. Don't take along any gold, silver, or copper coins. And don't carry a traveling bag or an extra shirt or sandals or a walking stick.

Workers deserve their food. So when you go to a town or a village, find someone worthy enough to have you as their guest and stay with them until you leave. When you go to a home, give it your blessing of peace. If the home is deserving, let your blessing remain with them. But if the home isn't deserving, take back your blessing of peace. If someone won't welcome you or listen to your message, leave their home or town. And shake the dust from your feet at them. I promise you that the day of judgment will be easier for the towns of Sodom and Gomorrah than for that town.

I am sending you like lambs into a pack of wolves. So be as wise as snakes and as innocent as doves. Watch out for people who will take you to court and have you beaten in their meeting places. Because of me, you will be dragged before rulers and kings to tell them and the Gentiles about your faith. But when someone arrests you, don't worry about what you will say or how you will say it. At that time you will be given the words to say. But you will not really be the one speaking. The Spirit from your Father will tell you what to say.

Brothers and sisters will betray one another and have each other put to death. Parents will betray their own children, and children will turn against their parents and have them killed. Everyone will hate you because of me. But if you remain faithful until the end, you will be saved. When people mistreat you in one town, hurry to another one. I promise you that before you have gone to all the towns of Israel, the Son of Man will come.

Disciples are not better than their teacher, and slaves are not better than their master. It is enough for disciples to be like their teacher and for slaves to be like their master. If people call the head of the family Satan, what will they say about the rest of the family?

Don't be afraid of anyone! Everything that is hidden will be found out, and every secret will be known. Whatever I say to you in the dark, you must tell in the light. And you must announce from the housetops whatever I have whispered to you. Don't be afraid of people. They can kill you, but they cannot harm your soul. Instead, you should fear God who can destroy both your body and your soul in hell. Aren't two sparrows sold for only a penny? But your Father knows when any one of them falls to the ground. Even the hairs on your head are counted. So don't be afraid! You are worth much more than many sparrows.

If you tell others that you belong to me, I will tell my Father in heaven that you are my followers. But if you reject me, I will tell my Father in heaven that you don't belong to me.

Don't think that I came to bring peace to the earth! I came to bring trouble, not peace. I came to turn sons against their fathers, daughters against their mothers, and daughters-in-law against their mothers-in-law. Your worst enemies will be in your own family.

If you love your father or mother or even your sons and daughters more than me, you are not fit to be my disciples. And unless you are willing to take up your cross and come with me, you are not fit to be my disciples. If you try to save your life, you will lose it. But if you give it up for me, you will surely find it.

Anyone who welcomes you welcomes me. And anyone who

welcomes me also welcomes the one who sent me. Anyone who welcomes a prophet, just because that person is a prophet, will be given the same reward as a prophet. Anyone who welcomes a good person, just because that person is good, will be given the same reward as a good person. And anyone who gives one of my most humble followers a cup of cool water, just because that person is my follower, will surely be rewarded. [57]

The apostles left and went from village to village,[58] and started telling everyone to turn to God. They forced out many demons and healed a lot of sick people by putting olive oil on them.[59]

After Jesus had finished instructing his twelve disciples, he left and began teaching and preaching in the towns. [60]

4.3 John the Baptist Beheaded

Jesus became so well-known that Herod the ruler heard about him. Some people thought he was John the Baptist, who had come back to life with the power to work miracles. Others thought he was Elijah or some other prophet who had lived long ago. But when Herod heard about Jesus, he said, "This must be John! I had his head cut off, and now he has come back to life. [61] That's why he has the power to work these miracles." [62]

Herod had earlier married Herodias, the wife of his brother Philip. But John had told him, "It isn't right for you to take your brother's wife!" So, in order to please Herodias, Herod arrested John and put him in prison.

Herodias had a grudge against John and wanted to kill him. But she could not do it because Herod was afraid of John and protected him. He knew that John was a good and holy man. Even though Herod was confused by what John said, he was glad to listen to him. And he often did.

Finally, Herodias got her chance when Herod gave a great birthday celebration for himself and invited his officials, his army officers, and the leaders of Galilee. The daughter of Herodias came in and danced for Herod and his guests. She pleased them so much that Herod said, "Ask for anything, and it's yours! I swear that I will give you as much as half of my kingdom, if you want it."

The girl left and asked her mother, "What do you think I should ask for?"

Her mother answered, "The head of John the Baptist!"

The girl hurried back and told Herod, "Right now on a platter I want the head of John the Baptist!"

The king was very sorry for what he had said. But he did not want to break the promise he had made in front of his guests. At once he ordered a guard to cut off John's head there in prison. The guard put the head on a platter and took it to the girl. Then she gave it to her mother.

When John's followers learned that he had been killed, they took his body and put it in a tomb.⁶³ Then they told Jesus what had happened.⁶⁴

 Jesus Feeds the Five Thousand

After the apostles returned to Jesus, they told him everything they had done and taught. But so many people were coming and going that Jesus and the apostles did not even have a chance to eat. Then Jesus said, "Let's go to a place where we can be alone and get some rest." They left in a boat for a place where they could be alone. But many people saw them leave and figured out where they were going. So people from every town ran on ahead and got there first.

When Jesus got out of the boat, he saw the large crowd that was like sheep without a shepherd. He felt sorry for the people and started teaching them many things.

That evening the disciples came to Jesus and said, "This place is like a desert, and it is already late. Let the crowds leave, so they can go to the farms and villages near here and buy something to eat."

Jesus replied, "You give them something to eat."⁶⁵

Philip answered, "Don't you know that it would take almost a year's wages just to buy only a little bread for each of these people?"

Andrew, the brother of Simon Peter, was one of the disciples. He spoke up and said, "There is a boy here who has five small loaves of barley bread and two fish. But what good is that with all these people?"

The ground was covered with grass, and Jesus told his disciples to have everyone sit down. About five thousand men were in the crowd. Jesus took the bread in his hands and gave thanks to God. Then he passed the bread to the people, and he did the same with the fish, until everyone had plenty to eat.

The people ate all they wanted, and Jesus told his disciples to gather up the leftovers, so that nothing would be wasted. The disciples gathered them up and filled twelve large baskets with what was left over from the five barley loaves.

After the people had seen Jesus work this miracle, they began saying, "This must be the Prophet who is to come into the world!" Jesus realized that they would try to force him to be their king. ⁶⁶

Right away, Jesus made his disciples get into the boat and start back across to Bethsaida. But he stayed until he had sent the crowds away. ⁶⁷

Then he went up on a mountain where he could be alone and pray.

4.5 Jesus Walks on the Water

Later that evening, he was still there.

By this time the boat was a long way from the shore. It was going against the wind and was being tossed around by the waves. A little while before morning, Jesus came walking on the water toward his disciples. When they saw him, they thought he was a ghost. They were terrified and started screaming.

At once, Jesus said to them, "Don't worry! I am Jesus. Don't be afraid."

Peter replied, "Lord, if it is really you, tell me to come to you on the water."

"Come on!" Jesus said. Peter then got out of the boat and started walking on the water toward him.

But when Peter saw how strong the wind was, he was afraid and started sinking. "Save me, Lord!" he shouted.

Right away, Jesus reached out his hand. He helped Peter up and said, "You surely don't have much faith. Why do you doubt?"

When Jesus and Peter got into the boat, the wind died down. The men in the boat worshiped Jesus and said, "You really are the Son of God!" [68]

4.6 Jesus Heals All Who Touch Him

Jesus and his disciples crossed the lake and brought the boat to shore near the town of Gennesaret. As soon as they got out of the boat, the people recognized Jesus. So they ran all over that part of the country to bring their sick people to him on mats. They brought them each time they heard where he was. In every village or farm or marketplace where Jesus went, the people brought their sick to him. They begged him to let them just touch his clothes, and everyone who did was healed. [69]

4.7 Jesus the Bread of Life

The people who had stayed on the east side of the lake knew that only one boat had been there. They also knew that Jesus had not left in it with his disciples. But the next day some boats from Tiberias sailed near the place where the crowd had eaten the bread for which the Lord had given thanks. They saw that Jesus and his disciples had left. Then they got into the boats and went to Capernaum to look for Jesus. They found him on the west side of the lake and asked, "Rabbi, when did you get here?"

Jesus answered, "I tell you for certain that you are not looking for me because you saw the miracles, but because you ate all the food you wanted. Don't work for food that spoils. Work for food that gives eternal life. The Son of Man will give you this food, because God the Father has given him the right to do so."

"What exactly does God want us to do?" the people asked.

Jesus answered, "God wants you to have faith in the one he sent."

They replied, "What miracle will you work, so that we can have faith in you? What will you do? For example, when our ancestors were in the desert, they were given manna to eat. It happened just as the Scriptures say, 'God gave them bread from heaven to eat.' "

Jesus then told them, "I tell you for certain that Moses wasn't the one who gave you bread from heaven. My Father is the one who gives you the true bread from heaven. And the bread that God gives is the one who came down from heaven to give life to the world."

The people said, "Lord, give us this bread and don't ever stop!"

Jesus replied:

> I am the bread that gives life! No one who comes to me will ever be hungry. No one who has faith in me will ever be thirsty. I have told you already that you have seen me and still do not have faith in me. Everything and everyone that the Father has given me will come to me, and I won't turn any of them away.
>
> I didn't come from heaven to do what I want! I came to do what the Father wants me to do. He sent me, and he wants to make certain that none of the ones he has given me will be lost. Instead, he wants me to raise them to life on the last day. My Father wants everyone who sees the Son to have faith in him and to have eternal life. Then I will raise them to life on the last day.

The people started grumbling because Jesus had said he was the bread that had come down from heaven. They were asking each other, "Isn't he Jesus, the son of Joseph? Don't we know his father and mother? How can he say that he has come down from heaven?"

Jesus told them:

> Stop grumbling! No one can come to me, unless the Father who sent me makes them want to come. But if they do come, I will raise them to life on the last day. One of the prophets wrote, 'God will teach all of them.' And so everyone who listens to the Father and learns from him will come to me.
>
> The only one who has seen the Father is the one who has come from him. No one else has ever seen the Father. I tell you for certain that everyone who has faith in me has eternal life.
>
> I am the bread that gives life! Your ancestors ate manna in the

desert, and later they died. But the bread from heaven has come down, so that no one who eats it will ever die. I am that bread from heaven! Everyone who eats it will live forever. My flesh is the life-giving bread that I give to the people of this world.

They started arguing with each other and asked, "How can he give us his flesh to eat?"

Jesus answered:

> I tell you for certain that you won't live unless you eat the flesh and drink the blood of the Son of Man. But if you do eat my flesh and drink my blood, you will have eternal life, and I will raise you to life on the last day. My flesh is the true food, and my blood is the true drink. If you eat my flesh and drink my blood, you are one with me, and I am one with you.
>
> The living Father sent me, and I have life because of him. Now everyone who eats my flesh will live because of me. The bread that comes down from heaven isn't like what your ancestors ate. They died, but whoever eats this bread will live forever.

Jesus was teaching in a Jewish place of worship in Capernaum when he said these things.

4.8 Many Disciples Leave Jesus

Many of Jesus' disciples heard him and said, "This is too hard for anyone to understand."

Jesus knew that his disciples were grumbling. So he asked, "Does this bother you? What if you should see the Son of Man go up to heaven where he came from? The Spirit is the one who gives life! Human strength can do nothing. The words that I have spoken to you are from that life-giving Spirit. But some of you refuse to have faith in me." Jesus said this, because from the beginning he knew who would have faith in him. He also knew which one would betray him.

Then Jesus said, "You cannot come to me, unless the Father makes you want to come. That is why I have told these things to all of you."

Because of what Jesus said, many of his disciples turned their backs on him and stopped following him. Jesus then asked his twelve disciples if they were going to leave him. Simon Peter answered, "Lord, there is no one else that we can go to! Your words give eternal life. We have faith in you, and we are sure that you are God's Holy One."

Jesus told his disciples, "I chose all twelve of you, but one of you is a demon!" Jesus was talking about Judas, the son of Simon Iscariot. He would later betray Jesus, even though he was one of the twelve disciples. Jesus decided to leave Judea and to start going through Galilee because the Jewish leaders wanted to kill him. [70]

4.9 Clean and Unclean

Some Pharisees and several teachers of the Law of Moses from Jerusalem came and gathered around Jesus. They noticed that some of his disciples ate without first washing their hands.

The Pharisees and many Jewish people obey the teachings of their ancestors. They always wash their hands in the proper way before eating. None of them will eat anything they buy in the market until it is washed. They also follow a lot of other teachings, such as washing cups, pitchers, and bowls.

The Pharisees and teachers asked Jesus, "Why don't your disciples obey what our ancestors taught us to do? Why do they eat without washing their hands?"

Jesus replied:

You are nothing but show-offs! The prophet Isaiah was right when he wrote that God had said,

> "All of you praise me with your words,
>   but you never really think about me.
> It is useless for you to worship me,
>   when you teach rules made up by humans."

You disobey God's commands in order to obey what humans have taught. You are good at rejecting God's commands so that you can follow your own teachings! Didn't Moses command you to respect your father and mother? Didn't he tell you to put to death all who curse their parents? But you let people get by without helping their parents when they should. You let them say that what they own has been offered to God. You won't let those people help their parents. And you ignore God's commands in order to follow your own teaching. You do a lot of other things that are just as bad.

Jesus called the crowd together again and said, "Pay attention and try to understand what I mean. The food that you put into your mouth doesn't make you unclean and unfit to worship God. The bad words that come out of your mouth are what make you unclean." [71]

Then his disciples came over to him and asked, "Do you know that you insulted the Pharisees by what you said?"

Jesus answered, "Every plant that my Father in heaven did not plant will be pulled up by the roots. Stay away from those Pharisees! They are like blind people leading other blind people, and all of them will fall into a ditch."

Peter replied, "What did you mean when you talked about the things that make people unclean?"

Jesus then said:

Don't any of you know what I am talking about by now? Don't you know that the food you put into your mouth goes into your stomach and then out of your body? But the words that come out of your mouth come from your heart. And they are what make you unfit to worship God. Out of your heart come evil thoughts, murder, unfaithfulness in marriage, vulgar deeds, stealing, telling lies, and insulting others. These are what make you unclean. Eating without washing your hands will not make you unfit to worship God.

4.10 The Faith of the Canaanite Woman

Jesus left and went to the territory near the cities of Tyre and Sidon. Suddenly a Canaanite woman from there came out shouting, "Lord and Son of David, have pity on me! My daughter is full of demons." Jesus did not say a word. But the woman kept following along and shouting, so his disciples came up and asked him to send her away.

Jesus said, "I was sent only to the people of Israel! They are like a flock of lost sheep."

The woman came closer. Then she knelt down and begged, "Please help me, Lord!"

Jesus replied, "It isn't right to take food away from children and feed it to dogs."

"Lord, that's true," the woman said, "but even dogs get the crumbs that fall from their owner's table."

Jesus answered, "Dear woman, you really do have a lot of faith, and you will be given what you want." At that moment her daughter was healed. [72]

4.11 The Healing of a Deaf and Mute Man

Jesus left the region around Tyre and went by way of Sidon toward Lake Galilee. He went through the land near the ten cities known as Decapolis. [73]

Large crowds came and brought many people who were crippled or blind or lame or unable to talk. They placed them, and many others, in front of Jesus, and he healed them all. [74]

Some people brought to him a man who was deaf and could hardly talk. They begged Jesus just to touch him.

After Jesus had taken him aside from the crowd, he stuck his fingers in the man's ears. Then he spit and put it on the man's tongue. Jesus looked up toward heaven, and with a groan he said, "Effatha!" which means "Open up!" At once the man could hear, and he had no more trouble talking clearly.

Jesus told the people not to say anything about what he had done. But the more he told them, the more they talked about it. [75]

Everyone was amazed at what they saw and heard. People who had never spoken could now speak. The lame were healed, the crippled could walk, and the blind were able to see. [76]

"Everything he does is good! He even heals people who cannot hear or talk." [77]

Everyone was praising the God of Israel.

4.12 Jesus Feeds the Four Thousand

Jesus called his disciples together and told them, "I feel sorry for these people. They have been with me for three days, and they don't have anything to eat. I don't want to send them away hungry. They might faint on their way home."

His disciples said, "This place is like a desert. Where can we find enough food to feed such a crowd?"

Jesus asked them how much food they had. They replied, "Seven small loaves of bread and a few little fish."

After Jesus had told the people to sit down, he took the seven loaves of bread and the fish and gave thanks. He then broke them and handed them to his disciples, who passed them around to the crowds.

Everyone ate all they wanted, and the leftovers filled seven large baskets.

There were four thousand men who ate, not counting the women and children.

After Jesus had sent the crowds away, he got into a boat and sailed across the lake. He came to shore near the town of Magadan.

4.13 The Demand for a Sign

The Pharisees and Sadducees came to Jesus and tried to test him by asking for a sign from heaven. He told them:

"If the sky is red in the evening, you say the weather will be good. But if the sky is red and gloomy in the morning, you say it is going to rain. You can tell what the weather will be like by looking at the sky. But you don't understand what is happening now. You want a sign because you are evil and won't believe! But the only sign you will be given is what happened to Jonah."

Then Jesus left.

4.14 The Yeast of the Pharisees and Sadducees

The disciples had forgotten to bring any bread when they crossed the lake. Jesus then warned them, "Watch out! Guard against the yeast of the Pharisees and Sadducees."

The disciples talked this over and said to each other, "He must be saying this because we didn't bring along any bread."

Jesus knew what they were thinking and said:

"You surely don't have much faith! Why are you talking about not having any bread? Don't you understand? Have you forgotten about the five thousand people and all those baskets of leftovers from just five loaves of bread? And what about the four thousand people and all those baskets of leftovers from only seven loaves of bread? Don't you know by now that I am not talking to you about bread? Watch out for the yeast of the Pharisees and Sadducees!"

Finally, the disciples understood that Jesus wasn't talking about the yeast used to make bread, but about the teaching of the Pharisees and Sadducees. [78]

4.15 The Healing of a Blind Man at Bethsaida

As Jesus and his disciples were going into Bethsaida, some people brought a blind man to him and begged him to touch the man. Jesus took him by the hand and led him out of the village, where he spit into the man's eyes. He placed his hands on the blind man and asked him if he could see anything. The man looked up and said, "I see people, but they look like trees walking around."

Once again Jesus placed his hands on the man's eyes, and this time the man stared. His eyes were healed, and he saw everything clearly. Jesus said to him, "You may return home now, but don't go into the village."[79]

4.16 Peter's Confession of Messiah

When Jesus and his disciples were near the town of Caesarea Philippi, he asked them, "What do people say about the Son of Man?"

The disciples answered, "Some people say you are John the Baptist or maybe Elijah or Jeremiah or some other prophet."

Then Jesus asked them, "But who do you say I am?"

Simon Peter spoke up, "You are the Messiah, the Son of the living God."

Jesus told him:

> Simon, son of Jonah, you are blessed! You didn't discover this on your own. It was shown to you by my Father in heaven. So I will call you Peter, which means 'a rock.' On this rock I will build my church, and death itself will not have any power over it. I will give you the keys to the kingdom of heaven, and God in heaven will allow whatever you allow on earth. But he will not allow anything that you don't allow.

Jesus told his disciples not to tell anyone that he was the Messiah.

4.17 Jesus Predicts His Death

From then on, Jesus began telling his disciples what would happen to him. He said, "I must go to Jerusalem. There the nation's leaders, the chief priests, and the teachers of the Law of Moses will make me suffer terribly. I will be killed, but three days later I will rise to life."

Peter took Jesus aside and told him to stop talking like that. He said, "God would never let this happen to you, Lord!"

Jesus turned to Peter and said, "Satan, get away from me! You're in my way because you think like everyone else and not like God."

Then Jesus said to his disciples:

> If any of you want to be my followers, you must forget about yourself. You must take up your cross and follow me. If you want to save your life, you will destroy it. But if you give up your life for me, you will find it. What will you gain, if you own the whole world but destroy yourself? What would you give to get back your soul? [80]
>
> If you are ashamed of me and my message, the Son of Man will be ashamed of you when he comes in his glory and in the glory of his Father and the holy angels [81] to reward all people for what they have done. I promise you that some of those standing here will not die before they see the Son of Man coming with his kingdom.

4.18 The Transfiguration

Six days later Jesus took Peter and the brothers James and John with him. They went up on a very high mountain where they could be alone [82] to pray. While he was praying, [83] there in front of the disciples, Jesus was completely changed. His face was shining like the sun, and his clothes became white as light. [84]

Suddenly Moses and Elijah were there speaking with him. They appeared in heavenly glory and talked about all that Jesus' death in Jerusalem would mean.

Peter and the other two disciples had been sound asleep. All at once they woke up and saw how glorious Jesus was. They also saw the two men who were with him.

Moses and Elijah were about to leave, when Peter said to Jesus, "Master, it is good for us to be here! Let us make three shelters, one for you, one for Moses, and one for Elijah." But Peter did not know what he was talking about. [85]

While Peter was still speaking, the shadow of a bright cloud passed over them. From the cloud a voice said, "This is my own dear Son, and I am pleased with him. Listen to what he says!" When the disciples heard the voice, they were so afraid that they fell flat on the ground. But Jesus came over and touched them. He said, "Get up and don't be afraid!" When they opened their eyes, they saw only Jesus.

On their way down from the mountain, Jesus warned his disciples not to tell anyone what they had seen until after the Son of Man had been raised from death.

The disciples asked Jesus, "Don't the teachers of the Law of Moses say that Elijah must come before the Messiah does?"

Jesus told them, "Elijah certainly will come and get everything ready. In fact, he has already come. But the people did not recognize him and treated him just as they wanted to. They will soon make the Son of Man suffer in the same way." Then the disciples understood that Jesus was talking to them about John the Baptist.

4.19 Jesus Heals a Boy With a Demon

Jesus and his disciples returned to the crowd. A man knelt in front of him and said, "Lord, have pity on my son! He has a bad case of epilepsy and often falls into a fire or into water. I brought him to your disciples, but none of them could heal him."

Jesus said, "You people are too stubborn to have any faith! How much longer must I be with you? Why do I have to put up with you? Bring the boy here." [86]

They brought the boy, and as soon as the demon saw Jesus, it made the boy shake all over. He fell down and began rolling on the ground and foaming at the mouth.

Jesus asked the boy's father, "How long has he been like this?"

The man answered, "Ever since he was a child. The demon has often tried to kill him by throwing him into a fire or into water. Please have pity and help us if you can!"

Jesus replied, "Why do you say 'if you can'? Anything is possible for someone who has faith!"

Right away the boy's father shouted, "I do have faith! Please help me to have even more."

When Jesus saw that a crowd was gathering fast, he spoke sternly to the evil spirit that had kept the boy from speaking or hearing. He said, "I order you to come out of the boy! Don't ever bother him again."

The spirit screamed and made the boy shake all over. Then it went out of him. The boy looked dead, and almost everyone said he was. But Jesus took hold of his hand and helped him stand up.

After Jesus and the disciples had gone back home and were alone, they asked him, "Why couldn't we force out that demon?"

Jesus answered, "Only prayer can force out that kind of demon."

4.20 Jesus Again Predicts His Death

Jesus left with his disciples and started through Galilee. He did not want anyone to know about it, because he was teaching the disciples that the Son of Man would be handed over to people who would kill him. But three days later he would rise to life. The disciples did not understand what Jesus meant, and they were afraid to ask. [87]

4.21 The Temple Tax

When Jesus and the others arrived in Capernaum, the collectors for the temple tax came to Peter and asked, "Does your teacher pay the temple tax?"

"Yes, he does," Peter answered.

After they had returned home, Jesus went up to Peter and asked him, "Simon, what do you think? Do the kings of this earth collect taxes and fees from their own people or from foreigners?"

Peter answered, "From foreigners."

Jesus replied, "Then their own people don't have to pay. But we don't want to cause trouble. So go cast a line into the lake and pull out the first fish you hook. Open its mouth, and you will find a coin. Use it to pay your taxes and mine."

4.22 The Greatest in the Kingdom of Heaven

About this time the disciples came to Jesus and asked him who would be the greatest in the kingdom of heaven. Jesus called a child over and had the child stand near him. Then he said:

I promise you this. If you don't change and become like a child, you will never get into the kingdom of heaven. But if you are as humble as this child, you are the greatest in the kingdom of heaven. And when you welcome one of these children because of me, you welcome me. [88]

John said, "Teacher, we saw a man using your name to force demons out of people. But he wasn't one of us, and we told him to stop."

Jesus said to his disciples:

> Don't stop him! No one who works miracles in my name will soon turn and say something bad about me. Anyone who isn't against us is for us. And anyone who gives you a cup of water in my name, just because you belong to me, will surely be rewarded. [89]
>
> It will be terrible for people who cause even one of my little followers to sin. Those people would be better off thrown into the deepest part of the ocean with a heavy stone tied around their neck! The world is in for trouble because of the way it causes people to sin. There will always be something to cause people to sin, but anyone who does this will be in for trouble.
>
> If your hand or foot causes you to sin, chop it off and throw it away! You would be better off to go into life crippled or lame than to have two hands or two feet and be thrown into the fire that never goes out. If your eye causes you to sin, poke it out and get rid of it. You would be better off to go into life with only one eye than to have two eyes and be thrown into the fires of hell.
>
> Don't be cruel to any of these little ones! I promise you that their angels are always with my Father in heaven. Let me ask you this. What would you do if you had a hundred sheep and one of them wandered off? Wouldn't you leave the ninety-nine on the hillside and go look for the one that had wandered away? I am sure that finding it would make you happier than having the ninety-nine that never wandered off. That's how it is with your Father in heaven. He doesn't want any of these little ones to be lost.

4.23 A Follower Who Sins Against You

> If one of my followers sins against you, go and point out what was wrong. But do it in private, just between the two of you. If that person listens, you have won back a follower. But if that one refuses to listen, take along one or two others. The Scriptures teach that every complaint must be proven true by two or more witnesses. If the follower refuses to listen to them, report the matter to the church. Anyone who refuses to listen to the church must be treated like an unbeliever or a tax collector.

I promise you that God in heaven will allow whatever you allow on earth, but he will not allow anything you don't allow. I promise that when any two of you on earth agree about something you are praying for, my Father in heaven will do it for you. Whenever two or three of you come together in my name, I am there with you.

4.24 The Parable of the Unmerciful Servant

Peter came up to the Lord and asked, "How many times should I forgive someone who does something wrong to me? Is seven times enough?" Jesus answered:

Not just seven times, but seventy-seven times! This story will show you what the kingdom of heaven is like:

One day a king decided to call in his officials and ask them to give an account of what they owed him. As he was doing this, one official was brought in who owed him fifty million silver coins. But he didn't have any money to pay what he owed. The king ordered him to be sold, along with his wife and children and all he owned, in order to pay the debt.

The official got down on his knees and began begging, "Have pity on me, and I will pay you every cent I owe!" The king felt sorry for him and let him go free. He even told the official that he did not have to pay back the money.

As the official was leaving, he happened to meet another official, who owed him a hundred silver coins. So he grabbed the man by the throat. He started choking him and said, "Pay me what you owe!"

The man got down on his knees and began begging, "Have pity on me, and I will pay you back." But the first official refused to have pity. Instead, he went and had the other official put in jail until he could pay what he owed.

When some other officials found out what had happened, they felt sorry for the man who had been put in jail. Then they told the king what had happened. The king called the first official back in and said, "You're an evil man! When you begged for mercy, I said you did not have to pay back a cent. Don't you think you should show pity to someone else, as I did to you?" The king was so angry that he ordered the official to be tortured until he could pay back everything he owed. That is how my Father in heaven will treat you, if you don't forgive each of my followers with all your heart. [90]

4.25 The Cost of Following Jesus

Along the way someone said to Jesus, "I'll go anywhere with you!"

Jesus said, "Foxes have dens, and birds have nests, but the Son of Man doesn't have a place to call his own."

Jesus told someone else to come with him. But the man said, "Lord, let me wait until I bury my father."

Jesus answered, "Let the dead take care of the dead, while you go and tell about God's kingdom."

Then someone said to Jesus, "I want to go with you, Lord, but first let me go back and take care of things at home."

Jesus answered, "Anyone who starts plowing and keeps looking back isn't worth a thing to God's kingdom!" [91]

4.26 Jesus Goes to the Festival of Shelters

It was almost time for the Festival of Shelters, and Jesus' brothers said to him, "Why don't you go to Judea? Then your disciples can see what you are doing. No one does anything in secret, if they want others to know about them. So let the world know what you are doing!" Even Jesus' own brothers had not yet become his followers.

Jesus answered, "My time hasn't yet come, but your time is always here. The people of this world cannot hate you. They hate me, because I tell them that they do evil things. Go on to the festival. My time hasn't yet come, and I am not going." Jesus said this and stayed on in Galilee.

After Jesus' brothers had gone to the festival, he went secretly, without telling anyone.

During the festival the Jewish leaders looked for Jesus and asked, "Where is he?" The crowds even got into an argument about him. Some were saying, "Jesus is a good man," while others were saying, "He is lying to everyone." But the people were afraid of their leaders, and none of them talked in public about him.

4.27 Jesus Teaches at the Festival

When the festival was about half over, Jesus went into the temple and started teaching. The leaders were surprised and said, "How does this man know so much? He has never been taught!"

Jesus replied:

I am not teaching something that I thought up. What I teach comes from the one who sent me. If you really want to obey God, you will know if what I teach comes from God or from me. If I wanted to bring honor to myself, I would speak for myself. But I want to honor the one who sent me. That is why I tell the truth and not a lie. Didn't Moses give you the Law? Yet none of you obey it! So why do you want to kill me?

The crowd replied, "You're crazy! What makes you think someone wants to kill you?"

Jesus answered:

> I worked one miracle, and it amazed you. Moses commanded you to circumcise your sons. But it wasn't really Moses who gave you this command. It was your ancestors, and even on the Sabbath you circumcise your sons in order to obey the Law of Moses. Why are you angry with me for making someone completely well on the Sabbath? Don't judge by appearances. Judge by what is right.

4.28 Is Jesus the Messiah?

Some of the people from Jerusalem were saying, "Isn't this the man they want to kill? Yet here he is, speaking for everyone to hear. And no one is arguing with him. Do you suppose the authorities know that he is the Messiah? But how could that be? No one knows where the Messiah will come from, but we know where this man comes from."

As Jesus was teaching in the temple, he shouted, "Do you really think you know me and where I came from? I didn't come on my own! The one who sent me is truthful, and you don't know him. But I know the one who sent me, because I came from him."

Some of the people wanted to arrest Jesus right then. But no one even laid a hand on him, because his time had not yet come. A lot of people in the crowd put their faith in him and said, "When the Messiah comes, he surely won't perform more miracles than this man has done!"

When the Pharisees heard the crowd arguing about Jesus, they got together with the chief priests and sent some temple police to arrest him. But Jesus told them, "I will be with you a little while longer, and then I will return to the one who sent me. You will look for me, but you won't find me. You cannot go where I am going."

The Jewish leaders asked each other, "Where can he go to keep us from finding him? Is he going to some foreign country where our people live? Is he going there to teach the Greeks? What did he mean by saying that we will look for him, but won't find him? Why can't we go where he is going?"

On the last and most important day of the festival, Jesus stood up and shouted, "If you are thirsty, come to me and drink! Have faith in me, and you will have life-giving water flowing from deep inside you, just as the

Scriptures say." Jesus was talking about the Holy Spirit, who would be given to everyone that had faith in him. The Spirit had not yet been given to anyone, since Jesus had not yet been given his full glory.

When the crowd heard Jesus say this, some of them said, "He must be the Prophet!" Others said, "He is the Messiah!" Others even said, "Can the Messiah come from Galilee? The Scriptures say that the Messiah will come from the family of King David. Doesn't this mean that he will be born in David's hometown of Bethlehem?" The people started taking sides against each other because of Jesus. Some of them wanted to arrest him, but no one laid a hand on him.

4.29 Unbelief of the Jewish Leaders

When the temple police returned to the chief priests and Pharisees, they were asked, "Why didn't you bring Jesus here?"

They answered, "No one has ever spoken like that man!"

The Pharisees said to them, "Have you also been fooled? Not one of the chief priests or the Pharisees has faith in him. And these people who don't know the Law are under God's curse anyway."

Nicodemus was there at the time. He was a member of the council, and was the same one who had earlier come to see Jesus. He said, "Our Law doesn't let us condemn people before we hear what they have to say. We cannot judge them before we know what they have done."

Then they said, "Nicodemus, you must be from Galilee! Read the Scriptures, and you will find that no prophet is to come from Galilee."

4.30 The Woman Caught in Adultery

Everyone else went home, but Jesus walked out to the Mount of Olives. Then early the next morning he went to the temple. The people came to him, and he sat down and started teaching them.

The Pharisees and the teachers of the Law of Moses brought in a woman who had been caught in bed with a man who wasn't her husband. They made her stand in the middle of the crowd. Then they said, "Teacher, this woman was caught sleeping with a man who isn't her husband. The Law of Moses teaches that a woman like this should be stoned to death! What do you say?"

They asked Jesus this question, because they wanted to test him and bring some charge against him. But Jesus simply bent over and started writing on the ground with his finger.

They kept on asking Jesus about the woman. Finally, he stood up and said, "If any of you have never sinned, then go ahead and throw the first stone at her!" Once again he bent over and began writing on the ground. The people left one by one, beginning with the oldest. Finally, Jesus and the woman were there alone.

Jesus stood up and asked her, "Where is everyone? Isn't there anyone left to accuse you?"

"No sir," the woman answered.

Then Jesus told her, "I am not going to accuse you either. You may go now, but don't sin anymore."

4.31 The Validity of Jesus' Testimony

Once again Jesus spoke to the people. This time he said, "I am the light for the world! Follow me, and you won't be walking in the dark. You will have the light that gives life."

The Pharisees objected, "You are the only one speaking for yourself, and what you say isn't true!"

Jesus replied:

> Even if I do speak for myself, what I say is true! I know where I came from and where I am going. But you don't know where I am from or where I am going. You judge in the same way that everyone else does, but I don't judge anyone. If I did judge, I would judge fairly, because I would not be doing it alone. The Father who sent me is here with me. Your Law requires two witnesses to prove that something is true. I am one of my witnesses, and the Father who sent me is the other one.

"Where is your Father?" they asked.

"You don't know me or my Father!" Jesus answered. "If you knew me, you would know my Father."

Jesus said this while he was still teaching in the place where the temple treasures were stored. But no one arrested him, because his time had not yet come.

Jesus also told them, "I am going away, and you will look for me. But you cannot go where I am going, and you will die with your sins unforgiven."

The Jewish leaders asked, "Does he intend to kill himself? Is that what he means by saying we cannot go where he is going?"

Jesus answered, "You are from below, but I am from above. You belong to this world, but I don't. That is why I said you will die with your sins unforgiven. If you don't have faith in me for who I am, you will die, and your sins will not be forgiven."

"Who are you?" they asked Jesus.

Jesus answered, "I am exactly who I told you at the beginning. There is a lot more I could say to condemn you. But the one who sent me is truthful, and I tell the people of this world only what I have heard from him."

No one understood that Jesus was talking to them about the Father.

Jesus went on to say, "When you have lifted up the Son of Man, you will know who I am. You will also know that I don't do anything on my own. I say only what my Father taught me. The one who sent me is with me. I always do what pleases him, and he will never leave me."

After Jesus said this, many of the people put their faith in him.

4.32 The Children of Abraham

Jesus told the people who had faith in him, "If you keep on obeying what I have said, you truly are my disciples. You will know the truth, and the truth will set you free."

They answered, "We are Abraham's children! We have never been anyone's slaves. How can you say we will be set free?"

Jesus replied:

> I tell you for certain that anyone who sins is a slave of sin! And slaves don't stay in the family forever, though the Son will always remain in the family. If the Son gives you freedom, you are free! I know that you are from Abraham's family. Yet you want to kill me, because my message isn't really in your hearts. I am telling you what my Father has shown me, just as you are doing what your father has taught you.

The people said to Jesus, "Abraham is our father!"

Jesus replied, "If you were Abraham's children, you would do what Abraham did. Instead, you want to kill me for telling you the truth that God gave me. Abraham never did anything like that. But you are doing exactly what your father does."

"Don't accuse us of having someone else as our father!" they said. "We just have one father, and he is God."

4.33 The Children of the Devil

Jesus answered:

> If God were your Father, you would love me, because I came from God and only from him. He sent me. I did not come on my own. Why can't you understand what I am talking about? Can't you stand to hear what I am saying? Your father is the devil, and you do exactly what he wants. He has always been a murderer and a liar. There is nothing

truthful about him. He speaks on his own, and everything he says is a lie. Not only is he a liar himself, but he is also the father of all lies.

Everything I have told you is true, and you still refuse to have faith in me. Can any of you accuse me of sin? If you cannot, why won't you have faith in me? After all, I am telling you the truth. Anyone who belongs to God will listen to his message. But you refuse to listen, because you don't belong to God."

4.34 The Claims of Jesus About Himself

The people told Jesus, "We were right to say that you are a Samaritan and that you have a demon in you!"

Jesus answered, "I don't have a demon in me. I honor my Father, and you refuse to honor me. I don't want honor for myself. But there is one who wants me to be honored, and he is also the one who judges. I tell you for certain that if you obey my words, you will never die."

Then the people said, "Now we are sure that you have a demon. Abraham is dead, and so are the prophets. How can you say that no one who obeys your words will ever die? Are you greater than our father Abraham? He died, and so did the prophets. Who do you think you are?"

Jesus replied, "If I honored myself, it would mean nothing. My Father is the one who honors me. You claim that he is your God, even though you don't really know him. If I said I didn't know him, I would be a liar, just like all of you. But I know him, and I do what he says. Your father Abraham was really glad to see me."

"You are not even fifty years old!" they said. "How could you have seen Abraham?"

Jesus answered, "I tell you for certain that even before Abraham was, I was, and I am." The people picked up stones to kill Jesus, but he hid and left the temple.

4.35 Jesus Heals a Man Born Blind

As Jesus walked along, he saw a man who had been blind since birth. Jesus' disciples asked, "Teacher, why was this man born blind? Was it because he or his parents sinned?"

"No, it wasn't!" Jesus answered. "But because of his blindness, you will see God work a miracle for him. As long as it is day, we must do what the one who sent me wants me to do. When night comes, no one can work. While I am in the world, I am the light for the world."

After Jesus said this, he spit on the ground. He made some mud and smeared it on the man's eyes. Then he said, "Go and wash off the mud in

Siloam Pool." The man went and washed in Siloam, which means "One Who Is Sent." When he had washed off the mud, he could see.

The man's neighbors and the people who had seen him begging wondered if he really could be the same man. Some of them said he was the same beggar, while others said he only looked like him. But he told them, "I am that man."

"Then how can you see?" they asked.

He answered, "Someone named Jesus made some mud and smeared it on my eyes. He told me to go and wash it off in Siloam Pool. When I did, I could see."

"Where is he now?" they asked.

"I don't know," he answered.

4.36 The Pharisees Investigate the Healing

The day when Jesus made the mud and healed the man was a Sabbath. So the people took the man to the Pharisees. They asked him how he was able to see, and he answered, "Jesus made some mud and smeared it on my eyes. Then after I washed it off, I could see."

Some of the Pharisees said, "This man Jesus doesn't come from God. If he did, he would not break the law of the Sabbath."

Others asked, "How could someone who is a sinner work such a miracle?"

Since the Pharisees could not agree among themselves, they asked the man, "What do you say about this one who healed your eyes?"

"He is a prophet!" the man told them.

But the Jewish leaders would not believe that the man had once been blind. They sent for his parents and asked them, "Is this the son that you said was born blind? How can he now see?"

The man's parents answered, "We are certain that he is our son, and we know that he was born blind. But we don't know how he got his sight or who gave it to him. Ask him! He is old enough to speak for himself."

The man's parents said this because they were afraid of the Jewish leaders. The leaders had already agreed that no one was to have anything to do with anyone who said Jesus was the Messiah.

The leaders called the man back and said, "Swear by God to tell the truth! We know that Jesus is a sinner."

The man replied, "I don't know if he is a sinner or not. All I know is that I used to be blind, but now I can see!"

"What did he do to you?" the Jewish leaders asked. "How did he heal your eyes?"

The man answered, "I have already told you once, and you refused to listen. Why do you want me to tell you again? Do you also want to become his disciples?"

The leaders insulted the man and said, "You are his follower! We are followers of Moses. We are sure that God spoke to Moses, but we don't even know where Jesus comes from."

"How strange!" the man replied. "He healed my eyes, and yet you don't know where he comes from. We know that God listens only to people who love and obey him. God doesn't listen to sinners. And this is the first time in history that anyone has ever given sight to someone born blind. Jesus could not do anything unless he came from God."

The leaders told the man, "You have been a sinner since the day you were born! Do you think you can teach us anything?" Then they said, "You can never come back into any of our meeting places!"

4.37 Spiritual Blindness

When Jesus heard what had happened, he went and found the man. Then Jesus asked, "Do you have faith in the Son of Man?"

He replied, "Sir, if you will tell me who he is, I will put my faith in him."

"You have already seen him," Jesus answered, "and right now he is talking with you."

The man said, "Lord, I put my faith in you!" Then he worshiped Jesus.

Jesus told him, "I came to judge the people of this world. I am here to give sight to the blind and to make blind everyone who can see."

When the Pharisees heard Jesus say this, they asked, "Are we blind?"

Jesus answered, "If you were blind, you would not be guilty. But now that you claim to see, you will keep on being guilty."

4.38 The Shepherd and His Flock

Jesus said:

I tell you for certain that only thieves and robbers climb over the fence instead of going in through the gate to the sheep pen. But the gatekeeper opens the gate for the shepherd, and he goes in through it. The sheep know their shepherd's voice. He calls each of them by name and leads them out.

When he has led out all of his sheep, he walks in front of them, and they follow, because they know his voice. The sheep will not follow strangers. They don't recognize a stranger's voice, and they run away.

Jesus told the people this story. But they did not understand what he was talking about.

Jesus said:

> I tell you for certain that I am the gate for the sheep. Everyone who came before me was a thief or a robber, and the sheep did not listen to any of them. I am the gate. All who come in through me will be saved. Through me they will come and go and find pasture.
>
> A thief comes only to rob, kill, and destroy. I came so that everyone would have life, and have it in its fullest. I am the good shepherd, and the good shepherd gives up his life for his sheep. Hired workers are not like the shepherd. They don't own the sheep, and when they see a wolf coming, they run off and leave the sheep. Then the wolf attacks and scatters the flock. Hired workers run away because they don't care about the sheep.
>
> I am the good shepherd. I know my sheep, and they know me. Just as the Father knows me, I know the Father, and I give up my life for my sheep. I have other sheep that are not in this sheep pen. I must bring them together too, when they hear my voice. Then there will be one flock of sheep and one shepherd.
>
> The Father loves me, because I give up my life, so that I may receive it back again. No one takes my life from me. I give it up willingly! I have the power to give it up and the power to receive it back again, just as my Father commanded me to do.

The people took sides because of what Jesus had told them. Many of them said, "He has a demon in him! He is crazy! Why listen to him?"

But others said, "How could anyone with a demon in him say these things? No one like that could give sight to a blind person!" [92]

4.39 Jesus Sends Out the Seventy-Two

Later the Lord chose seventy-two other followers and sent them out two by two to every town and village where he was about to go. He said to them:

> A large crop is in the fields, but there are only a few workers. Ask the Lord in charge of the harvest to send out workers to bring it in. Now go, but remember, I am sending you like lambs into a pack of wolves. Don't take along a moneybag or a traveling bag or sandals. And don't waste time greeting people on the road. As soon as you enter a home, say, "God bless this home with peace." If the people living there

are peace-loving, your prayer for peace will bless them. But if they are not peace-loving, your prayer will return to you. Stay with the same family, eating and drinking whatever they give you, because workers are worth what they earn. Don't move around from house to house.

If the people of a town welcome you, eat whatever they offer. Heal their sick and say, "God's kingdom will soon be here!"

But if the people of a town refuse to welcome you, go out into the street and say, "We are shaking the dust from our feet as a warning to you. And you can be sure that God's kingdom will soon be here!" I tell you that on the day of judgment the people of Sodom will get off easier than the people of that town!

You people of Chorazin are in for trouble! You people of Bethsaida are also in for trouble! If the miracles that took place in your towns had happened in Tyre and Sidon, the people there would have turned to God long ago. They would have dressed in sackcloth and put ashes on their heads. On the day of judgment the people of Tyre and Sidon will get off easier than you will. People of Capernaum, do you think you will be honored in heaven? Well, you will go down to hell!

My followers, whoever listens to you is listening to me. Anyone who says "No" to you is saying "No" to me. And anyone who says "No" to me is really saying "No" to the one who sent me.

When the seventy-two followers returned, they were excited and said, "Lord, even the demons obeyed when we spoke in your name!"

Jesus told them:

I saw Satan fall from heaven like a flash of lightning. I have given you the power to trample on snakes and scorpions and to defeat the power of your enemy Satan. Nothing can harm you. But don't be happy because evil spirits obey you. Be happy that your names are written in heaven!

At that same time, Jesus felt the joy that comes from the Holy Spirit, and he said:

My Father, Lord of heaven and earth, I am grateful that you hid all this from wise and educated people and showed it to ordinary people. Yes, Father, that is what pleased you.

My Father has given me everything, and he is the only one who knows the Son. The only one who really knows the Father is the Son. But the Son wants to tell others about the Father, so that they can know him too.

Jesus then turned to his disciples and said to them in private, "You are really blessed to see what you see! Many prophets and kings were eager to see what you see and to hear what you hear. But I tell you that they did not see or hear."

4.40 The Parable of the Good Samaritan

An expert in the Law of Moses stood up and asked Jesus a question to see what he would say. "Teacher," he asked, "what must I do to have eternal life?"

Jesus answered, "What is written in the Scriptures? How do you understand them?"

The man replied, "The Scriptures say, 'Love the Lord your God with all your heart, soul, strength, and mind.' They also say, 'Love your neighbors as much as you love yourself.' "

Jesus said, "You have given the right answer. If you do this, you will have eternal life."

But the man wanted to show that he knew what he was talking about. So he asked Jesus, "Who are my neighbors?"

Jesus replied:

> As a man was going down from Jerusalem to Jericho, robbers attacked him and grabbed everything he had. They beat him up and ran off, leaving him half dead.
>
> A priest happened to be going down the same road. But when he saw the man, he walked by on the other side. Later a temple helper came to the same place. But when he saw the man who had been beaten up, he also went by on the other side.
>
> A man from Samaria then came traveling along that road. When he saw the man, he felt sorry for him and went over to him. He treated his wounds with olive oil and wine and bandaged them. Then he put him on his own donkey and took him to an inn, where he took care of him. The next morning he gave the innkeeper two silver coins and said, "Please take care of the man. If you spend more than this on him, I will pay you when I return."

Then Jesus asked, "Which one of these three people was a real neighbor to the man who was beaten up by robbers?"

The teacher answered, "The one who showed pity."

Jesus said, "Go and do the same!"

4.41 At the Home of Martha and Mary

The Lord and his disciples were traveling along and came to a village. When they got there, a woman named Martha welcomed him into her home. She had a sister named Mary, who sat down in front of the Lord and was listening to what he said. Martha was worried about all that had to be done. Finally, she went to Jesus and said, "Lord, doesn't it bother you that my sister has left me to do all the work by myself? Tell her to come and help me!"

The Lord answered, "Martha, Martha! You are worried and upset about so many things, but only one thing is necessary. Mary has chosen what is best, and it will not be taken away from her."

4.42 Jesus' Teaching on Prayer

When Jesus had finished praying, one of his disciples said to him, "Lord, teach us to pray, just as John taught his followers to pray."
So Jesus told them, "Pray in this way:

'Father, help us to honor your name.
   Come and set up your kingdom.
Give us each day the food we need.
Forgive our sins,
   as we forgive everyone who has done wrong to us.
And keep us from being tempted.' "

Then Jesus went on to say:

Suppose one of you goes to a friend in the middle of the night and says, "Let me borrow three loaves of bread. A friend of mine has dropped in, and I don't have a thing for him to eat." And suppose your friend answers, "Don't bother me! The door is bolted, and my children and I are in bed. I cannot get up to give you something."

He may not get up and give you the bread, just because you are his friend. But he will get up and give you as much as you need, simply because you are not ashamed to keep on asking.

So I tell you to ask and you will receive, search and you will find, knock and the door will be opened for you. Everyone who asks will receive, everyone who searches will find, and the door will be opened for everyone who knocks. Which one of you fathers would give your hungry child a snake if the child asked for a fish? Which one of you would give your child a scorpion if the child asked for an egg? As bad as you are, you still know how to give good gifts to your children. But your heavenly Father is even more ready to give the Holy Spirit to anyone who asks. [93]

4.43 Jesus Accuses the Pharisees and the Teachers of the Law

When Jesus finished speaking, a Pharisee invited him home for a meal. Jesus went and sat down to eat. The Pharisee was surprised that he did not wash his hands before eating. So the Lord said to him:

You Pharisees clean the outside of cups and dishes, but on the inside you are greedy and evil. You fools! Didn't God make both the outside and the inside? If you would only give what you have to the poor, everything you do would please God.

You Pharisees are in for trouble! You give God a tenth of the spices from your gardens, such as mint and rue. But you cheat people, and you don't love God. You should be fair and kind to others and still give a tenth to God.

You Pharisees are in for trouble! You love the front seats in the meeting places, and you like to be greeted with honor in the market. But you are in for trouble! You are like unmarked graves that people walk on without even knowing it.

A teacher of the Law of Moses spoke up, "Teacher, you said cruel things about us."

Jesus replied:

You teachers are also in for trouble! You load people down with heavy burdens, but you won't lift a finger to help them carry the loads. Yes, you are really in for trouble. You build monuments to honor the prophets your own people murdered long ago. You must think that was the right thing for your people to do, or else you would not have built monuments for the prophets they murdered.

Because of your evil deeds, the Wisdom of God said, 'I will send prophets and apostles to you. But you will murder some and mistreat others.' You people living today will be punished for all the prophets who have been murdered since the beginning of the world. This includes every prophet from the time of Abel to the time of Zechariah, who was murdered between the altar and the temple. You people will certainly be punished for all of this.

You teachers of the Law of Moses are really in for trouble! You carry the keys to the door of knowledge about God. But you never go in, and you keep others from going in.

Jesus was about to leave, but the teachers and the Pharisees wanted to get even with him. They tried to make him say what he thought about other things, so that they could catch him saying something wrong.

4.44 Warnings and Encouragements

As thousands of people crowded around Jesus and were stepping on each other, he told his disciples:

Be sure to guard against the dishonest teaching of the Pharisees! It is their way of fooling people. Everything that is hidden will be found out, and every secret will be known. Whatever you say in the dark will be heard when it is day. Whatever you whisper in a closed room will be shouted from the housetops.

My friends, don't be afraid of people. They can kill you, but after that, there is nothing else they can do. God is the one you must fear. Not only can he take your life, but he can throw you into hell. God is certainly the one you should fear!

Five sparrows are sold for just two pennies, but God doesn't forget a one of them. Even the hairs on your head are counted. So don't be afraid! You are worth much more than many sparrows.

If you tell others that you belong to me, the Son of Man will tell God's angels that you are my followers. But if you reject me, you will be rejected in front of them. If you speak against the Son of Man, you can be forgiven, but if you speak against the Holy Spirit, you cannot be forgiven.

When you are brought to trial in the Jewish meeting places or before rulers or officials, don't worry about how you will defend yourselves or what you will say. At that time the Holy Spirit will tell you what to say.

4.45 The Parable of the Rich Fool

A man in a crowd said to Jesus, "Teacher, tell my brother to give me my share of what our father left us when he died."

Jesus answered, "Who gave me the right to settle arguments between you and your brother?"

Then he said to the crowd, "Don't be greedy! Owning a lot of things won't make your life safe."

So Jesus told them this story:

A rich man's farm produced a big crop, and he said to himself, "What can I do? I don't have a place large enough to store everything."

Later, he said, "Now I know what I'll do. I'll tear down my barns and build bigger ones, where I can store all my grain and other goods." Then I'll say to myself, "You have stored up enough good things to last for years to come. Live it up! Eat, drink, and enjoy yourself."

But God said to him, "You fool! Tonight you will die. Then who will get what you have stored up?"

This is what happens to people who store up everything for themselves, but are poor in the sight of God." [94]

4.46 Not Peace but Division

"I came to set fire to the earth, and I wish it were already on fire! I am going to be put to a hard test. And I will have to suffer a lot of pain until it is over. Do you think that I came to bring peace to earth? No indeed! I came to make people choose sides. A family of five will be divided, with two of them against the other three. Fathers and sons will turn against one another, and mothers and daughters will do the same. Mothers-in-law and daughters-in-law will also turn against each other." [95]

4.47 Repent or Perish

About this same time Jesus was told that Pilate had given orders for some people from Galilee to be killed while they were offering sacrifices. Jesus replied:

Do you think that these people were worse sinners than everyone else in Galilee just because of what happened to them? Not at all! But you can be sure that if you don't turn back to God, every one of you will also be killed. What about those eighteen people who died when the tower in Siloam fell on them? Do you think they were worse than everyone else in Jerusalem? Not at all! But you can be sure that if you don't turn back to God, every one of you will also die.

Jesus then told them this story:

A man had a fig tree growing in his vineyard. One day he went out to pick some figs, but he didn't find any. So he said to the gardener, "For three years I have come looking for figs on this tree, and I haven't found any yet. Chop it down! Why should it take up space?"

The gardener answered, "Master, leave it for another year. I'll dig around it and put some manure on it to make it grow. Maybe it will have figs on it next year. If it doesn't, you can have it cut down."

4.48 A Crippled Woman Healed on the Sabbath

One Sabbath, Jesus was teaching in a Jewish meeting place, and a woman was there who had been crippled by an evil spirit for eighteen years.

She was completely bent over and could not straighten up. When Jesus saw the woman, he called her over and said, "You are now well." He placed his hands on her, and right away she stood up straight and praised God.

The man in charge of the meeting place was angry because Jesus had healed someone on the Sabbath. So he said to the people, "Each week has six days when we can work. Come and be healed on one of those days, but not on the Sabbath."

The Lord replied, "Are you trying to fool someone? Won't any one of you untie your ox or donkey and lead it out to drink on a Sabbath? This woman belongs to the family of Abraham, but Satan has kept her bound for eighteen years. Isn't it right to set her free on the Sabbath?" Jesus' words made his enemies ashamed. But everyone else in the crowd was happy about the wonderful things he was doing.[96]

4.49 The Unbelief of the Jews

That winter, Jesus was in Jerusalem for the Temple Festival. One day he was walking in that part of the temple known as Solomon's Porch, and the people gathered all around him. They said, "How long are you going to keep us guessing? If you are the Messiah, tell us plainly!"

Jesus answered:

> I have told you, and you refused to believe me. The things I do by my Father's authority show who I am. But since you are not my sheep, you don't believe me. My sheep know my voice, and I know them. They follow me, and I give them eternal life, so that they will never be lost. No one can snatch them out of my hand. My Father gave them to me, and he is greater than all others. No one can snatch them from his hands, and I am one with the Father.

Once again the Jewish leaders picked up stones in order to kill Jesus. But he said, "I have shown you many good things that my Father sent me to do. Which one are you going to stone me for?"

They answered, "We are not stoning you because of any good thing you did. We are stoning you because you did a terrible thing. You are just a man, and here you are claiming to be God!"

Jesus replied:

> In your Scriptures doesn't God say, "You are gods"? You can't argue with the Scriptures, and God spoke to those people and called them gods. So why do you accuse me of a terrible sin for saying that I am the Son of God? After all, it is the Father who prepared me for this work. He is also the one who sent me into the world. If I don't do as my Father does, you should not believe me. But if I do what my

Father does, you should believe because of that, even if you don't have faith in me. Then you will know for certain that the Father is one with me, and I am one with the Father.

Again they wanted to arrest Jesus. But he escaped and crossed the Jordan to the place where John had earlier been baptizing. While Jesus was there, many people came to him. They were saying, "John didn't work any miracles, but everything he said about Jesus is true." A lot of those people also put their faith in Jesus. [97]

4.50 The Narrow Door

As Jesus was on his way to Jerusalem, he taught the people in the towns and villages. Someone asked him, "Lord, are only a few people going to be saved?"

Jesus answered:

Do all you can to go in by the narrow door! A lot of people will try to get in, but will not be able to. Once the owner of the house gets up and locks the door, you will be left standing outside. You will knock on the door and say, "Sir, open the door for us!"

But the owner will answer, "I don't know a thing about you!"

Then you will start saying, "We dined with you, and you taught in our streets."

But he will say, "I really don't know who you are! Get away from me, you evil people!"

Then when you have been thrown outside, you will weep and grit your teeth because you will see Abraham, Isaac, Jacob, and all the prophets in God's kingdom. People will come from all directions and sit down to feast in God's kingdom. There the ones who are now least important will be the most important, and those who are now most important will be least important.

4.51 Jesus' Sorrow for Jerusalem

At that time some Pharisees came to Jesus and said, "You had better get away from here! Herod wants to kill you."

Jesus said to them:

Go tell that fox, "I am going to force out demons and heal people today and tomorrow, and three days later I'll be through." But I am going on my way today and tomorrow and the next day. After all, Jerusalem is the place where prophets are killed.

Jerusalem, Jerusalem! Your people have killed the prophets and have stoned the messengers who were sent to you. I have often

wanted to gather your people, as a hen gathers her chicks under her wings. But you wouldn't let me. Now your temple will be deserted. You won't see me again until the time when you say,
"Blessed is the one who comes
   in the name of the Lord."

4.52 Jesus at a Pharisee's House

One Sabbath, Jesus was having dinner in the home of an important Pharisee, and everyone was carefully watching Jesus. All of a sudden a man with swollen legs stood up in front of him. Jesus turned and asked the Pharisees and the teachers of the Law of Moses, "Is it right to heal on the Sabbath?" But they did not say a word.

Jesus took hold of the man. Then he healed him and sent him away. Afterwards, Jesus asked the people, "If your son or ox falls into a well, wouldn't you pull him out right away, even on the Sabbath?" There was nothing they could say.

Jesus saw how the guests had tried to take the best seats. So he told them:

When you are invited to a wedding feast, don't sit in the best place. Someone more important may have been invited. Then the one who invited you will come and say, "Give your place to this other guest!" You will be embarrassed and will have to sit in the worst place.

When you are invited to be a guest, go and sit in the worst place. Then the one who invited you may come and say, "My friend, take a better seat!" You will then be honored in front of all the other guests. If you put yourself above others, you will be put down. But if you humble yourself, you will be honored.

Then Jesus said to the man who had invited him:

When you give a dinner or a banquet, don't invite your friends and family and relatives and rich neighbors. If you do, they will invite you in return, and you will be paid back. When you give a feast, invite the poor, the crippled, the lame, and the blind. They cannot pay you back. But God will bless you and reward you when his people rise from death.

4.53 The Parable of the Great Banquet

After Jesus had finished speaking, one of the guests said, "The greatest blessing of all is to be at the banquet in God's kingdom!"
Jesus told him:

A man once gave a great banquet and invited a lot of guests. When the banquet was ready, he sent a servant to tell the guests, 'Everything is ready! Please come.'

One guest after another started making excuses. The first one said, 'I bought some land, and I've got to look it over. Please excuse me.'

Another guest said, 'I bought five teams of oxen, and I need to try them out. Please excuse me.'

Still another guest said, 'I have just gotten married, and I can't be there.'

The servant told his master what happened, and the master became so angry that he said, 'Go as fast as you can to every street and alley in town! Bring in everyone who is poor or crippled or blind or lame.'

When the servant returned, he said, 'Master, I've done what you told me, and there is still plenty of room for more people.'

His master then told him, 'Go out along the back roads and fence rows and make people come in, so that my house will be full. Not one of the guests I first invited will get even a bite of my food!'

4.54 The Cost of Being a Disciple

Large crowds were walking along with Jesus, when he turned and said:

You cannot be my disciple, unless you love me more than you love your father and mother, your wife and children, and your brothers and sisters. You cannot come with me unless you love me more than you love your own life.

You cannot be my disciple unless you carry your own cross and come with me.

Suppose one of you wants to build a tower. What is the first thing you will do? Won't you sit down and figure out how much it will cost and if you have enough money to pay for it? Otherwise, you will start building the tower, but not be able to finish. Then everyone who sees what is happening will laugh at you. They will say, "You started building, but could not finish the job."

What will a king do if he has only ten thousand soldiers to defend himself against a king who is about to attack him with twenty thousand soldiers? Before he goes out to battle, won't he first sit down and decide if he can win? If he thinks he won't be able to defend himself, he will send messengers and ask for peace while the other king is still a long way off. So then, you cannot be my disciple unless you give away everything you own.

Salt is good, but if it no longer tastes like salt, how can it be made to taste salty again? It is no longer good for the soil or even for the manure pile. People simply throw it out. If you have ears, pay attention!

4.55 The Parable of the Lost Sheep

Tax collectors and sinners were all crowding around to listen to Jesus. So the Pharisees and the teachers of the Law of Moses started grumbling, "This man is friendly with sinners. He even eats with them."

Then Jesus told them this story:

If any of you has a hundred sheep, and one of them gets lost, what will you do? Won't you leave the ninety-nine in the field and go look for the lost sheep until you find it? And when you find it, you will be so glad that you will put it on your shoulder and carry it home. Then you will call in your friends and neighbors and say, "Let's celebrate! I've found my lost sheep."

Jesus said, "In the same way there is more happiness in heaven because of one sinner who turns to God than over ninety-nine good people who don't need to."

4.56 The Parable of the Lost Coin

Jesus told the people another story:

What will a woman do if she has ten silver coins and loses one of them? Won't she light a lamp, sweep the floor, and look carefully until she finds it? Then she will call in her friends and neighbors and say, 'Let's celebrate! I've found the coin I lost.'"

Jesus said, "In the same way God's angels are happy when even one person turns to him."

4.57 The Parable of the Lost Son

Jesus also told them another story:

Once a man had two sons. The younger son said to his father, "Give me my share of the property." So the father divided his property between his two sons.

Not long after that, the younger son packed up everything he owned and left for a foreign country, where he wasted all his money in wild living. He had spent everything, when a bad famine spread through that whole land. Soon he had nothing to eat.

He went to work for a man in that country, and the man sent him out to take care of his pigs. He would have been glad to eat what the pigs were eating, but no one gave him a thing.

Finally, he came to his senses and said, "My father's workers have plenty to eat, and here I am, starving to death! I will go to my father and say to him, 'Father, I have sinned against God in heaven and against you. I am no longer good enough to be called your son. Treat me like one of your workers.' "

The younger son got up and started back to his father. But when he was still a long way off, his father saw him and felt sorry for him. He ran to his son and hugged and kissed him.

The son said, "Father, I have sinned against God in heaven and against you. I am no longer good enough to be called your son."

But his father said to the servants, "Hurry and bring the best clothes and put them on him. Give him a ring for his finger and sandals for his feet. Get the best calf and prepare it, so we can eat and celebrate. This son of mine was dead, but has now come back to life. He was lost and has now been found." And they began to celebrate.

The older son had been out in the field. But when he came near the house, he heard the music and dancing. So he called one of the servants over and asked, "What's going on here?"

The servant answered, "Your brother has come home safe and sound, and your father ordered us to kill the best calf." The older brother got so angry that he would not even go into the house.

His father came out and begged him to go in. But he said to his father, "For years I have worked for you like a slave and have always obeyed you. But you have never even given me a little goat, so that I could give a dinner for my friends. This other son of yours wasted your money on prostitutes. And now that he has come home, you ordered the best calf to be killed for a feast."

His father replied, "My son, you are always with me, and everything I have is yours. But we should be glad and celebrate! Your brother was dead, but he is now alive. He was lost and has now been found."

4.58 The Parable of the Dishonest Manager

Jesus said to his disciples:

A rich man once had a manager to take care of his business. But he was told that his manager was wasting money. So the rich man called him in and said, "What is this I hear about you? Tell me what you have done! You are no longer going to work for me."

The manager said to himself, "What shall I do now that my master is going to fire me? I can't dig ditches, and I'm ashamed to beg. I know what I'll do, so that people will welcome me into their homes after I've lost my job."

Then one by one he called in the people who were in debt to his master. He asked the first one, "How much do you owe my master?"

"A hundred barrels of olive oil," the man answered.

So the manager said, "Take your bill and sit down and quickly write 'fifty'."

The manager asked someone else who was in debt to his master, "How much do you owe?"

"A thousand bushels of wheat," the man replied.

The manager said, "Take your bill and write 'eight hundred'."

The master praised his dishonest manager for looking out for himself so well. That's how it is! The people of this world look out for themselves better than the people who belong to the light.

My disciples, I tell you to use wicked wealth to make friends for yourselves. Then when it is gone, you will be welcomed into an eternal home. Anyone who can be trusted in little matters can also be trusted in important matters. But anyone who is dishonest in little matters will be dishonest in important matters. If you cannot be trusted with this wicked wealth, who will trust you with true wealth? And if you cannot be trusted with what belongs to someone else, who will give you something that will be your own? You cannot be the slave of two masters. You will like one more than the other or be more loyal to one than to the other. You cannot serve God and money.

The Pharisees really loved money. So when they heard what Jesus said, they made fun of him. But Jesus told them:

You are always making yourselves look good, but God sees what is in your heart. The things that most people think are important are worthless as far as God is concerned.[98]

4.59 The Rich Man and Lazarus

There was once a rich man who wore expensive clothes and every day ate the best food. But a poor beggar named Lazarus was brought to the gate of the rich man's house. He was happy just to eat the scraps that fell from the rich man's table. His body was covered with sores, and dogs kept coming up to lick them. The poor man died, and angels took him to the place of honor next to Abraham.

The rich man also died and was buried. He went to hell and was suffering terribly. When he looked up and saw Abraham far off and Lazarus at his side, he said to Abraham, "Have pity on me! Send Lazarus to dip his finger in water and touch my tongue. I'm suffering terribly in this fire."

Abraham answered, "My friend, remember that while you lived, you had everything good, and Lazarus had everything bad. Now he is happy, and you are in pain. And besides, there is a deep ditch between us, and no one from either side can cross over."

But the rich man said, "Abraham, then please send Lazarus to my father's home. Let him warn my five brothers, so they won't come to this horrible place."

Abraham answered, "Your brothers can read what Moses and the prophets wrote. They should pay attention to that."

Then the rich man said, "No, that's not enough! If only someone from the dead would go to them, they would listen and turn to God."

So Abraham said, "If they won't pay attention to Moses and the prophets, they won't listen even to someone who comes back from the dead."

4.60 Sin, Faith and Duty

Jesus said to his disciples:
There will always be something that causes people to sin. But anyone who causes them to sin is in for trouble. A person who causes even one of my little followers to sin would be better off thrown into the ocean with a heavy stone tied around their neck. So be careful what you do.

Correct any followers of mine who sin, and forgive the ones who say they are sorry. Even if one of them mistreats you seven times in one day and says, "I am sorry," you should still forgive that person.
The apostles said to the Lord, "Make our faith stronger!"
Jesus replied:

If you had faith no bigger than a tiny mustard seed, you could tell this mulberry tree to pull itself up, roots and all, and to plant itself in the ocean. And it would!

If your servant comes in from plowing or from taking care of the sheep, would you say, "Welcome! Come on in and have something to eat?" No, you wouldn't say that. You would say, "Fix me something to eat. Get ready to serve me, so I can have my meal. Then later on you can eat and drink." Servants don't deserve special thanks for doing what they are supposed to do. And that's how it should be with you. When you've done all you should, then say, "We are merely servants, and we have simply done our duty." [99]

4.61 The Death of Lazarus

A man by the name of Lazarus was sick in the village of Bethany. He had two sisters, Mary and Martha. This was the same Mary who later poured perfume on the Lord's head and wiped his feet with her hair. The sisters sent a message to the Lord and told him that his good friend Lazarus was sick.

When Jesus heard this, he said, "His sickness won't end in death. It will bring glory to God and his Son."

Jesus loved Martha and her sister and brother. But he stayed where he was for two more days. Then he said to his disciples, "Now we will go back to Judea."

"Teacher," they said, "the people there want to stone you to death! Why do you want to go back?"

Jesus answered, "Aren't there twelve hours in each day? If you walk during the day, you will have light from the sun, and you won't stumble. But if you walk during the night, you will stumble, because you don't have any light." Then he told them, "Our friend Lazarus is asleep, and I am going there to wake him up."

They replied, "Lord, if he is asleep, he will get better." Jesus really meant that Lazarus was dead, but they thought he was talking only about sleep.

Then Jesus told them plainly, "Lazarus is dead! I am glad that I wasn't there, because now you will have a chance to put your faith in me. Let's go to him."

Thomas, whose nickname was "Twin," said to the other disciples, "Come on. Let's go, so we can die with him."

4.62 Jesus Comforts the Sisters

When Jesus got to Bethany, he found that Lazarus had already been in the tomb four days. Bethany was only about two miles from Jerusalem, and many people had come from the city to comfort Martha and Mary because their brother had died.

When Martha heard that Jesus had arrived, she went out to meet him, but Mary stayed in the house. Martha said to Jesus, "Lord, if you had been here, my brother would not have died. Yet even now I know that God will do anything you ask."

Jesus told her, "Your brother will live again!"

Martha answered, "I know that he will be raised to life on the last day, when all the dead are raised."

Jesus then said, "I am the one who raises the dead to life! Everyone who has faith in me will live, even if they die. And everyone who lives because of faith in me will never really die. Do you believe this?"

"Yes, Lord!" she replied. "I believe that you are Christ, the Son of God. You are the one we hoped would come into the world."

After Martha said this, she went and privately said to her sister Mary, "The Teacher is here, and he wants to see you." As soon as Mary heard this, she got up and went out to Jesus. He was still outside the village where Martha had gone to meet him. Many people had come to comfort Mary, and when they saw her quickly leave the house, they thought she was going out to the tomb to cry. So they followed her.

Mary went to where Jesus was. Then as soon as she saw him, she knelt at his feet and said, "Lord, if you had been here, my brother would not have died."

When Jesus saw that Mary and the people with her were crying, he was terribly upset and asked, "Where have you put his body?"

They replied, "Lord, come and you will see."

Jesus started crying, and the people said, "See how much he loved Lazarus."

Some of them said, "He gives sight to the blind. Why couldn't he have kept Lazarus from dying?"

4.63 Jesus Raises Lazarus from the Dead

Jesus was still terribly upset. So he went to the tomb, which was a cave with a stone rolled against the entrance. Then he told the people to roll the stone away. But Martha said, "Lord, you know that Lazarus has been dead four days, and there will be a bad smell."

Jesus replied, "Didn't I tell you that if you had faith, you would see the glory of God?"

After the stone had been rolled aside, Jesus looked up toward heaven and prayed, "Father, I thank you for answering my prayer. I know that you always answer my prayers. But I said this, so that the people here would believe that you sent me."

When Jesus had finished praying, he shouted, "Lazarus, come out!" The man who had been dead came out. His hands and feet were wrapped with strips of burial cloth, and a cloth covered his face.

Jesus then told the people, "Untie him and let him go."

4.64 The Plot to Kill Jesus

Many of the people who had come to visit Mary saw the things that Jesus did, and they put their faith in him. Others went to the Pharisees and told what Jesus had done. Then the chief priests and the Pharisees called the council together and said, "What should we do? This man is working a lot of miracles. If we don't stop him now, everyone will put their faith in him. Then the Romans will come and destroy our temple and our nation."

One of the council members was Caiaphas, who was also high priest that year. He spoke up and said, "You people don't have any sense at all! Don't you know it is better for one person to die for the people than for the whole nation to be destroyed?" Caiaphas did not say this on his own. As high priest that year, he was prophesying that Jesus would die for the nation. Yet Jesus would not die just for the Jewish nation. He would die to bring together all of God's scattered people. From that day on, the council started making plans to put Jesus to death.

Because of this plot against him, Jesus stopped going around in public. He went to the town of Ephraim, which was near the desert, and he stayed there with his disciples. [100]

4.65 Ten Men With Leprosy

On his way to Jerusalem, Jesus went along the border between Samaria and Galilee. As he was going into a village, ten men with leprosy came toward him. They stood at a distance and shouted, "Jesus, Master, have pity on us!"

Jesus looked at them and said, "Go show yourselves to the priests."

On their way they were healed. When one of them discovered that he was healed, he came back, shouting praises to God. He bowed down at the feet of Jesus and thanked him. The man was from the country of Samaria.

Jesus asked, "Weren't ten men healed? Where are the other nine? Why was this foreigner the only one who came back to thank God?" Then Jesus told the man, "You may get up and go. Your faith has made you well."

4.66 The Coming of the Kingdom of God

Some Pharisees asked Jesus when God's kingdom would come. He answered, "God's kingdom isn't something you can see. There is no use saying,

'Look! Here it is' or 'Look! There it is.' God's kingdom is here with you."
Jesus said to his disciples:

>The time will come when you will long to see one of the days of the Son of Man, but you will not. When people say to you, "Look there," or "Look here," don't go looking for him. The day of the Son of Man will be like lightning flashing across the sky. But first he must suffer terribly and be rejected by the people of today. When the Son of Man comes, things will be just as they were when Noah lived. People were eating, drinking, and getting married right up to the day when Noah went into the big boat. Then the flood came and drowned everyone on earth.
>
>When Lot lived, people were also eating and drinking. They were buying, selling, planting, and building. But on the very day Lot left Sodom, fiery flames poured down from the sky and killed everyone. The same will happen on the day when the Son of Man appears.
>
>At that time no one on a rooftop should go down into the house to get anything. No one in a field should go back to the house for anything. Remember what happened to Lot's wife.
>
>People who try to save their lives will lose them, and those who lose their lives will save them. On that night two people will be sleeping in the same bed, but only one will be taken. The other will be left. Two women will be together grinding wheat, but only one will be taken. The other will be left.

Then Jesus' disciples spoke up, "But where will this happen, Lord?" Jesus said, "Where there is a corpse, there will always be buzzards."

4.67 The Parable of the Persistent Widow

Jesus told his disciples a story about how they should keep on praying and never give up:

>In a town there was once a judge who didn't fear God or care about people. In that same town there was a widow who kept going to the judge and saying, "Make sure that I get fair treatment in court."
>
>For a while the judge refused to do anything. Finally, he said to himself, "Even though I don't fear God or care about people, I will help this widow because she keeps on bothering me. If I don't help her, she will wear me out."

The Lord said:

>Think about what that crooked judge said. Won't God

protect his chosen ones who pray to him day and night? Won't he be concerned for them? He will surely hurry and help them. But when the Son of Man comes, will he find on this earth anyone with faith?

4.68 The Parable of the Pharisee and the Tax Collector

Jesus told a story to some people who thought they were better than others and who looked down on everyone else:

Two men went into the temple to pray. One was a Pharisee and the other a tax collector. The Pharisee stood over by himself and prayed, "God, I thank you that I am not greedy, dishonest, and unfaithful in marriage like other people. And I am really glad that I am not like that tax collector over there. I go without eating for two days a week, and I give you one tenth of all I earn."

The tax collector stood off at a distance and did not think he was good enough even to look up toward heaven. He was so sorry for what he had done that he pounded his chest and prayed, "God, have pity on me! I am such a sinner."

Then Jesus said, "When the two men went home, it was the tax collector and not the Pharisee who was pleasing to God. If you put yourself above others, you will be put down. But if you humble yourself, you will be honored." [101]

4.69 Jesus' Teaching on Divorce

Some Pharisees wanted to test Jesus. They came up to him and asked, "Is it right for a man to divorce his wife for just any reason?"

Jesus answered, "Don't you know that in the beginning the Creator made a man and a woman? That's why a man leaves his father and mother and gets married. He becomes like one person with his wife. Then they are no longer two people, but one. And no one should separate a couple that God has joined together."

The Pharisees asked Jesus, "Why did Moses say that a man could write out divorce papers and send his wife away?"

Jesus replied, "You are so heartless! That's why Moses allowed you to divorce your wife. But from the beginning God did not intend it to be that way."[102]

When Jesus and his disciples were back in the house, they asked him about what he had said. He told them, "A man who divorces his wife and marries someone else is unfaithful to his wife. A woman who divorces her husband and marries again is also unfaithful." [103]

The disciples said, "If that's how it is between a man and a woman, it's better not to get married."

Jesus told them, "Only those people who have been given the gift of staying single can accept this teaching. Some people are unable to marry because of birth defects or because of what someone has done to their bodies. Others stay single for the sake of the kingdom of heaven. Anyone who can accept this teaching should do so." [104]

4.70 The Little Children and Jesus

Some people brought their children to Jesus so that he could bless them by placing his hands on them. But his disciples told the people to stop bothering him.

When Jesus saw this, he became angry and said, "Let the children come to me! Don't try to stop them. People who are like these little children belong to the kingdom of God. I promise you that you cannot get into God's kingdom, unless you accept it the way a child does." Then Jesus took the children in his arms and blessed them by placing his hands on them. [105]

4.71 The Rich Young Man

A man came to Jesus and asked, "Teacher, what good thing must I do to have eternal life?"

Jesus said to him, "Why do you ask me about what is good? Only God is good. If you want to have eternal life, you must obey his commandments."

"Which ones?" the man asked.

Jesus answered, "Do not murder. Be faithful in marriage. Do not steal. Do not tell lies about others. Respect your father and mother. And love others as much as you love yourself." [106]

The man answered, "Teacher, I have obeyed all these commandments since I was a young man."

Jesus looked closely at the man. He liked him and said, "There's one thing you still need to do. [107] If you want to be perfect, go sell everything you own! Give the money to the poor, and you will have riches in heaven. Then come and be my follower." When the young man heard this, he was sad, because he was very rich.

Jesus said to his disciples, "It's terribly hard for rich people to get into the kingdom of heaven! In fact, it's easier for a camel to go through the eye of a needle than for a rich person to get into God's kingdom."

When the disciples heard this, they were greatly surprised and asked, "How can anyone ever be saved?"

Jesus looked straight at them and said, "There are some things that people cannot do, but God can do anything."

Peter replied, "Remember, we have left everything to be your followers! What will we get?"

Jesus answered:

Yes, all of you have become my followers. And so in the future world, when the Son of Man sits on his glorious throne, I promise that you will sit on twelve thrones to judge the twelve tribes of Israel. All who have given up home or brothers and sisters or father and mother or children or land for me will be given a hundred times as much. They will also have eternal life. But many who are now first will be last, and many who are last will be first.

4.72 The Parable of the Workers in the Vineyard

As Jesus was telling what the kingdom of heaven would be like, he said:

Early one morning a man went out to hire some workers for his vineyard. After he had agreed to pay them the usual amount for a day's work, he sent them off to his vineyard.

About nine that morning, the man saw some other people standing in the market with nothing to do. He said he would pay them what was fair, if they would work in his vineyard. So they went.

At noon and again about three in the afternoon he returned to the market. And each time he made the same agreement with others who were loafing around with nothing to do.

Finally, about five in the afternoon the man went back and found some others standing there. He asked them, "Why have you been standing here all day long doing nothing?"

"Because no one has hired us," they answered. Then he told them to go work in his vineyard.

That evening the owner of the vineyard told the man in charge of the workers to call them in and give them their money. He also told the man to begin with the ones who were hired last. When the workers arrived, the ones who had been hired at five in the afternoon were given a full day's pay.

The workers who had been hired first thought they would be given more than the others. But when they were given the same, they began complaining to the owner of the vineyard. They said, "The ones who were hired last worked for only one hour. But you paid them the same that you did us. And we worked in the hot sun all day long!"

The owner answered one of them, "Friend, I didn't cheat you. I paid you exactly what we agreed on. Take your money now and go! What business is it of yours if I want to pay them the same that I paid you? Don't I have the right to do what I want with my own money? Why should you be jealous, if I want to be generous?"

Jesus then said, "So it is. Everyone who is now first will be last, and everyone who is last will be first." [108]

 ### Jesus Again Predicts His Death

Jesus took the twelve apostles aside and said:

We are now on our way to Jerusalem. Everything that the prophets wrote about the Son of Man will happen there. He will be handed over to foreigners, who will make fun of him, mistreat him, and spit on him. They will beat him and kill him, but three days later he will rise to life.

The apostles did not understand what Jesus was talking about. They could not understand, because the meaning of what he said was hidden from them. [109]

 ### A Mother's Request

The mother of James and John came to Jesus with her two sons. She knelt down and started begging him to do something for her. Jesus asked her what she wanted, and she said, "When you come into your kingdom, please let one of my sons sit at your right side and the other at your left."

Jesus answered, "Not one of you knows what you are asking. Are you able to drink from the cup that I must soon drink from?"

James and John said, "Yes, we are!"

Jesus replied, "You certainly will drink from my cup! But it isn't for me to say who will sit at my right side and at my left. That is for my Father to say."

When the ten other disciples heard this, they were angry with the two brothers. But Jesus called the disciples together and said:

You know that foreign rulers like to order their people around. And their great leaders have full power over everyone they rule. But don't act like them. If you want to be great, you must be the servant of all the others. And if you want to be first, you must be the slave of the rest. The Son of Man did not come to be a slave master, but a slave who will give his life to rescue many people. [110]

4.75 Blind Bartimaeus Receives His Sight

Jesus and his disciples went to Jericho. And as they were leaving, they were followed by a large crowd. A blind beggar by the name of Bartimaeus son of Timaeus was sitting beside the road. When he heard that it was Jesus from Nazareth, he shouted, "Jesus, Son of David, have pity on me!" Many people told the man to stop, but he shouted even louder, "Son of David, have pity on me!"

Jesus stopped and said, "Call him over!"

They called out to the blind man and said, "Don't be afraid! Come on! He is calling for you." The man threw off his coat as he jumped up and ran to Jesus.

Jesus asked, "What do you want me to do for you?"

The blind man answered, "Master, I want to see!"

Jesus told him, "You may go. Your eyes are healed because of your faith."

Right away the man could see, and he went down the road with Jesus. [111]

 ## 4.76 Zacchaeus the Tax Collector

Jesus was going through Jericho, where a man named Zacchaeus lived. He was in charge of collecting taxes and was very rich. Jesus was heading his way, and Zacchaeus wanted to see what he was like. But Zacchaeus was a short man and could not see over the crowd. So he ran ahead and climbed up into a sycamore tree.

When Jesus got there, he looked up and said, "Zacchaeus, hurry down! I want to stay with you today." Zacchaeus hurried down and gladly welcomed Jesus.

Everyone who saw this started grumbling, "This man Zacchaeus is a sinner! And Jesus is going home to eat with him."

Later that day Zacchaeus stood up and said to the Lord, "I will give half of my property to the poor. And I will now pay back four times as much to everyone I have ever cheated."

Jesus said to Zacchaeus, "Today you and your family have been saved, because you are a true son of Abraham. The Son of Man came to look for and to save people who are lost."

 ## 4.77 The Parable of the Ten Servants

The crowd was still listening to Jesus as he was getting close to Jerusalem. Many of them thought that God's kingdom would soon appear, and Jesus told them this story:

> A prince once went to a foreign country to be crowned king and then to return. But before leaving, he called in ten servants and gave each of them some money. He told them, "Use this to earn more money until I get back."
>
> But the people of his country hated him, and they sent messengers to the foreign country to say, "We don't want this man to be our king."
>
> After the prince had been made king, he returned and called in his servants. He asked them how much they had earned with the money they had been given.
>
> The first servant came and said, "Sir, with the money you gave me I have earned ten times as much."
>
> "That's fine, my good servant!" the king said. "Since you have shown that you can be trusted with a small amount, you will be given ten cities to rule."
>
> The second one came and said, "Sir, with the money you gave me, I have earned five times as much."
>
> The king said, "You will be given five cities."
>
> Another servant came and said, "Sir, here is your money. I kept it safe in a handkerchief. You are a hard man, and I was afraid of you. You take what isn't yours, and you harvest crops you didn't plant."
>
> "You worthless servant!" the king told him. "You have condemned yourself by what you have just said. You knew that I am a hard man, taking what isn't mine and harvesting what I've not planted. Why didn't you put my money in the bank? On my return, I could have had the money together with interest."
>
> Then he said to some other servants standing there, "Take the money away from him and give it to the servant who earned ten times as much."
>
> But they said, "Sir, he already has ten times as much!"
>
> The king replied, "Those who have something will be given more. But everything will be taken away from those who don't have anything. Now bring me the enemies who didn't want me to be their king. Kill them while I watch!"

When Jesus had finished saying all this, he went on toward Jerusalem. [112]

4.78 Mary Anoints Jesus at Bethany

It was almost time for Passover. Many of the Jewish people who lived out in the country had come to Jerusalem to get themselves ready for the festival. They looked around for Jesus. Then when they were in the temple, they asked each other, "You don't think he will come here for Passover, do you?"

The chief priests and the Pharisees told the people to let them know if any of them saw Jesus. That is how they hoped to arrest him.

Six days before Passover Jesus went back to Bethany, where he had raised Lazarus from death. A meal had been prepared for Jesus [113] at the home of Simon, who had leprosy. [114] Martha was doing the serving, and Lazarus himself was there.

Mary took a very expensive bottle of perfume and poured it on Jesus' feet. She wiped them with her hair, and the sweet smell of the perfume filled the house.

A disciple named Judas Iscariot was there. He was the one who was going to betray Jesus, and he asked, "Why wasn't this perfume sold for three hundred silver coins and the money given to the poor?" Judas did not really care about the poor. He asked this because he carried the moneybag and sometimes would steal from it. [115]

But Jesus said:

> Leave her alone! Why are you bothering her? She has done a beautiful thing for me. You will always have the poor with you. And whenever you want to, you can give to them. But you won't always have me here with you. She has done all she could by pouring perfume on my body to prepare it for burial. You may be sure that wherever the good news is told all over the world, people will remember what she has done. And they will tell others. [116]

A lot of people came when they heard that Jesus was there. They also wanted to see Lazarus, because Jesus had raised him from death. So the chief priests made plans to kill Lazarus. He was the reason that many of the Jewish people were turning from them and putting their faith in Jesus.

> "Lose your temper and you lose a friend; lie and you lose yourself."
> **Hopi**

REVIEW QUESTIONS, SECTION 4

1. Jesus saw the crowds as _____ without a shepherd. (4.1)

2. The apostles told people to turn to _____. (4.2)

3. Jesus said "My Father wants everyone who sees the Son to have _____ in Him and have _____ _____." (4.7)

4. Those who praised God with their words but never really think about God were called _____ by Jesus. (4.9)

5. People were completely amazed about Jesus, and said, "Everything He does is _____." (4.11)

6. Simon Peter said about Jesus, "You are the _____ the Son of the living God." (4.16)

7. Jesus asked His disciples, "What will you gain if you own the whole world but destroy _____?" (4.17)

8. What command concerning the Son did the voice from heaven give to Peter, James and John? _____ to what He says. (4.18)

9. Jesus told the father of the boy with a demon that _____ is possible for him who has faith. (4.19)

10. Did Jesus pay the temple tax? Yes ____ No___ (4.21)

11. Jesus taught that unless we change and become like a _____ we will never get into the kingdom of heaven. (4.22)

12. The Father in heaven is not willing that any of these little ones be _____. (4.22)

13. No one who looks _____ after starting to plow is worth a thing to the kingdom of God. (4.25)

14. Jesus said: "if you are thirsty, _____to me and drink." (4.28)

15. Those who have faith in Jesus will have _____ water flowing from deep inside of them. (4.28)

16. Did Jesus condemned the woman caught in adultery? Yes ___ No ___ He then said to her, "You may go now but don't _____ anymore." (4.30)

17. Jesus told the Jews who had believed Him, "If you keep on obeying what I have said you will know the truth, and the truth will _____ you _____ .(4.32)

18. "The one thing the man born blind knew for sure was, I used to be _____ but now I _____!" (4.36)

19. When Jesus was talking to His disciples about sheep, He said "I am the gate, all who come through Me will be _____ ."(4.38)

20. Jesus described himself by means of two comparisons with shepherding, "I am the good _____ for the sheep." and "the good shepherd gives up his _____ for the sheep." (4.38)

21. After the seventy-two returned, Jesus said to them, "But don't be happy because evil spirits obey you. Be happy that your _____ are written in_____." (4.39)

22. Jesus reaffirmed that we should love the Lord our God with all our _____ , _____ , _____ , and _____ and love our _____ as much as we love ourselves. (4.40)

23. Fathers know how to give their children _____ _____, but the Father in heaven gives the _____ _____ to those who ask Him. (4.42)

24. Jesus told the Pharisee who had invited Him to eat with him that being clean outside is of little worth if inside you are _____ and _____. (4.43)

25. Jesus said if you tell others you belong to Me, the Son of Man will tell God's angels that you are My _____. But if you reject Me you will be _____ in front of them. (4.44)

26. The woman that that had been crippled by an evil spirit for 18 years stood up _____ and _____ God after Jesus healed her. (4.48)

27. To those who insisted that he tell them plainly if he was the Christ, Jesus answered that they did not believe what He had already told them because they were not His _____. Then He explained to them that "My sheep know my _____. They _____ me, and I will give them _____ life, so that they shall never be lost." (4.49)

28. When the same unbelieving Jews accused Him of a terrible sin, Jesus said, "If I do what My Father does, you should _____ because of that." (4.49)

29. While Jesus made His way to Jerusalem, He was asked if only a few people were going to be saved. He told them to do all you can to go through the _____ door. (4.50)

30. At a Pharisee's house, Jesus told a story to illustrate that if you _____ yourself, you will be honored. (4.52)

31. Anyone who wants to be a disciple of Jesus must first _____ the cost just as one who wants to build a tower. (4.54)

32. There is happiness in heaven over one _____ who turns to God. (4.56)

33. Abraham told the rich man who was in hell that if his brothers did not pay attention to the Word of God they already knew (Moses and the Prophets), they would not _____ even if someone came back from the dead. (4.59)

34. In front of Lazarus' grave, Jesus declared, "I am the one who raises the dead to life. Everyone who has _____ in Me will live." (4.62)

35. One of the ten lepers Jesus healed, returned to Jesus and _____ Him when he realized he was healed. (4.65)

36. Through the parable of the Pharisee and the tax collector, Jesus taught that in order to be pleasing to God you must be _____ for what you have done and ask God to have _____ on you. (4.68)

37. When Jesus told the rich young man that only _____ is good, He implied that men are not good by nature. (4.71)

38. Jesus said they would _____ Him and _____ Him, but that three days later He would _____ to life. (4.73)

39. Jesus told His disciples, "If you want to be great you must be the _____." (4.74)

40. To Zacchaeus Jesus said, "The Son of Man came to look for and to _____ people who are lost." (4.76)

> Soon there will come from the rising of the sun a different kind of man from any you have yet seen, who will bring with them Leaves of Life and will teach you every thing.
> **Yureerachen, Spokane**

5 The Passion Week

5.1 The Triumphal Entry

The next day a large crowd was in Jerusalem for the Passover, and they heard that Jesus was coming for the festival.[117] As he was getting near Bethphage and Bethany on the Mount of Olives, he sent two of his disciples on ahead. He told them, "Go into the next village, where you will find a young donkey that has never been ridden. Untie the donkey and bring it here. If anyone asks why you are doing that, just say, 'The Lord needs it.' "

They went off and found everything just as Jesus had said. While they were untying the donkey, its owners asked, "Why are you doing that?"

They answered, "The Lord needs it."

Then they led the donkey to Jesus. They put some of their clothes on its back and helped Jesus get on. And as he rode along,[118] many people spread clothes on the road, while others went to cut branches from the fields.

In front of Jesus and behind him, people went along shouting,

"Hooray!
God bless the one who comes
   in the name of the Lord!
God bless the coming kingdom
   of our ancestor David.
Hooray for God
   in heaven above!" [119]

When Jesus was starting down the Mount of Olives, his large crowd of disciples were happy and praised God because of all the miracles they had seen. They shouted,

"Blessed is the king who comes
   in the name of the Lord!
Peace in heaven
   and glory to God."

Some Pharisees in the crowd said to Jesus, "Teacher, make your disciples stop shouting!"

But Jesus answered, "If they keep quiet, these stones will start shouting."

When Jesus came closer and could see Jerusalem, he cried and said:

It is too bad that today your people don't know what will bring them peace! Now it is hidden from them. Jerusalem, the time will come when your enemies will build walls around you to attack you. Armies will surround you and close in on you from every side. They will level you to the ground and kill your people. Not one stone in your buildings will be left on top of another. This will happen because you did not see that God had come to save you. [120]

When Jesus came to Jerusalem, everyone in the city was excited and asked, "Who can this be?"

The crowd answered, "This is Jesus, the prophet from Nazareth in Galilee." [121]

Blind and lame people came to Jesus in the temple, and he healed them. But the chief priests and the teachers of the Law of Moses were angry when they saw his miracles and heard the children shouting praises to the Son of David. The men said to Jesus, "Don't you hear what those children are saying?"

"Yes, I do!" Jesus answered. "Don't you know that the Scriptures say, 'Children and infants will sing praises?' " Then Jesus left the city and went out to the village of Bethany, where he spent the night.[122]

5.2 Jesus Curses the Fig Tree

When Jesus and his disciples left Bethany the next morning, he was hungry. From a distance Jesus saw a fig tree covered with leaves, and he went to see if there were any figs on the tree. But there were not any, because it wasn't the season for figs. So Jesus said to the tree, "Never again will anyone eat fruit from this tree!" The disciples heard him say this.

5.3 Jesus Again Clears the Temple

After Jesus and his disciples reached Jerusalem, he went into the temple and began chasing out everyone who was selling and buying. He turned over the tables of the moneychangers and the benches of those who were selling doves. Jesus would not let anyone carry things through the temple. Then he taught the people and said, "The Scriptures say, 'My house should be called a place of worship for all nations.' But you have made it a place where robbers hide!" [123]

Each day, Jesus kept on teaching in the temple. So the chief priests, the teachers of the Law of Moses, and some other important people tried to have him killed. But they could not find a way to do it, because everyone else was eager to listen to him. [124]

5.4 Jesus Once More Predicts His Death

Some Greeks had gone to Jerusalem to worship during Passover. Philip from Bethsaida in Galilee was there too. So they went to him and said, "Sir, we would like to meet Jesus." Philip told Andrew. Then the two of them went to Jesus and told him.

Jesus said:

> The time has come for the Son of Man to be given his glory. I tell you for certain that a grain of wheat that falls on the ground will never be more than one grain unless it dies. But if it dies, it will produce lots of wheat. If you love your life, you will lose it. If you give it up in this world, you will be given eternal life. If you serve me, you must go with me. My servants will be with me wherever I am. If you serve me, my Father will honor you.
>
> Now I am deeply troubled, and I don't know what to say. But I must not ask my Father to keep me from this time of suffering. In fact, I came into the world to suffer. So Father, bring glory to yourself.

A voice from heaven then said, "I have already brought glory to myself, and I will do it again!" When the crowd heard the voice, some of them thought it was thunder. Others thought an angel had spoken to Jesus.

Then Jesus told the crowd, "That voice spoke to help you, not me. This world's people are now being judged, and the ruler of this world is already being thrown out! If I am lifted up above the earth, I will make everyone want to come to me." Jesus was talking about the way he would be put to death.

The crowd said to Jesus, "The Scriptures teach that the Messiah will live forever. How can you say that the Son of Man must be lifted up? Who is this Son of Man?"

Jesus answered, "The light will be with you for only a little longer. Walk in the light while you can. Then you won't be caught walking blindly in the dark. Have faith in the light while it is with you, and you will be children of the light."

5.5 The Jews Continue in Their Unbelief

After Jesus had said these things, he left and went into hiding. He had worked a lot of miracles among the people, but they were still not willing to have faith in him. This happened so that what the prophet Isaiah had said would come true,

"Lord, who has believed
   our message?
And who has seen
   your mighty strength?"

The people could not have faith in Jesus, because Isaiah had also said,

"The Lord has blinded the eyes of the people,
   and he has made the people stubborn.
He did this so that they could not see or understand,
and so that they would not turn to the Lord
   and be healed."

Isaiah said this, because he saw the glory of Jesus and spoke about him. Even then, many of the leaders put their faith in Jesus, but they did not tell anyone about it. The Pharisees had already given orders for the people not to have anything to do with anyone who had faith in Jesus. And besides, the leaders liked praise from others more than they liked praise from God.

In a loud voice Jesus said:

   Everyone who has faith in me also has faith in the one who sent me. And everyone who has seen me has seen the one who sent me. I am the light that has come into the world. No one who has faith in me will stay in the dark.

   I am not the one who will judge those who refuse to obey my teachings. I came to save the people of this world, not to be their judge. But everyone who rejects me and my teachings will be judged on the last day by what I have said. I don't speak on my own. I say only what the Father who sent me has told me to say. I know that his commands will bring eternal life. That is why I tell you exactly what the Father has told me.[125]

That evening, Jesus and the disciples went outside the city.

5.6 The Fig Tree Withers

As the disciples walked past the fig tree the next morning, they noticed that it was completely dried up, roots and all. Peter remembered what Jesus had said to the tree. Then Peter said, "Teacher, look! The tree you put a curse on has dried up."

Jesus told his disciples:

> Have faith in God! If you have faith in God and don't doubt, you can tell this mountain to get up and jump into the sea, and it will. Everything you ask for in prayer will be yours, if you only have faith.
>
> Whenever you stand up to pray, you must forgive what others have done to you. Then your Father in heaven will forgive your sins.

5.7 The Authority of Jesus Questioned

Jesus and his disciples returned to Jerusalem. And as he was walking through the temple, the chief priests, the nation's leaders, and the teachers of the Law of Moses came over to him. They asked, "What right do you have to do these things? Who gave you this authority?"

Jesus answered, "I have just one question to ask you. If you answer it, I will tell you where I got the right to do these things. Who gave John the right to baptize? Was it God in heaven or merely some human being?"

They thought it over and said to each other, "We can't say that God gave John this right. Jesus will ask us why we didn't believe John. On the other hand, these people think that John was a prophet. So we can't say that it was merely some human who gave John the right to baptize."

They were afraid of the crowd and told Jesus, "We don't know."

Jesus replied, "Then I won't tell you who gave me the right to do what I do." [126]

5.8 The Parable of the Two Sons

Jesus said:

> I will tell you a story about a man who had two sons. Then you can tell me what you think. The father went to the older son and said, 'Go work in the vineyard today!' His son told him that he would not do it, but later he changed his mind and went. The man then told his younger son to go work in the vineyard. The boy said he would, but he didn't go. Which one of the sons obeyed his father?

"The older one," the chief priests and leaders answered.

Then Jesus told them:

You can be sure that tax collectors and prostitutes will get into the kingdom of God before you ever will! When John the Baptist showed you how to do right, you would not believe him. But these evil people did believe. And even when you saw what they did, you still would not change your minds and believe.

5.9 The Parable of the Renters

Jesus told the chief priests and leaders to listen to this story:

A land owner once planted a vineyard. He built a wall around it and dug a pit to crush the grapes in. He also built a lookout tower. Then he rented out his vineyard and left the country. [127]

When it was harvest time, he sent a servant to get his share of the grapes. The renters grabbed the servant. They beat him up and sent him away without a thing.

The owner sent another servant, but the renters beat him on the head and insulted him terribly. Then the man sent another servant, and they killed him. He kept sending servant after servant. They beat some of them and killed others.

The owner had a son he loved very much. Finally, he sent his son to the renters because he thought they would respect him. But they said to themselves, "Someday he will own this vineyard. Let's kill him! That way we can have it all for ourselves." So they grabbed the owner's son and killed him. Then they threw his body out of the vineyard. [128]

Jesus asked, "When the owner of that vineyard comes, what do you suppose he will do to those renters?"

The chief priests and leaders answered, "He will kill them in some horrible way. Then he will rent out his vineyard to people who will give him his share of grapes at harvest time."

Jesus replied, "You surely know that the Scriptures say,

'The stone that the builders tossed aside
    is now the most important stone of all.
This is something the Lord has done,
    and it is amazing to us.'

I tell you that God's kingdom will be taken from you and given to people who will do what he demands. Anyone who stumbles over this stone will be crushed, and anyone it falls on will be smashed to pieces."

When the chief priests and the Pharisees heard these stories, they knew that Jesus was talking about them. So they looked for a way to arrest

Jesus. But they were afraid to, because the people thought he was a prophet.

5.10 The Parable of the Wedding Banquet

Once again Jesus used stories to teach the people:

The kingdom of heaven is like what happened when a king gave a wedding banquet for his son. The king sent some servants to tell the invited guests to come to the banquet, but the guests refused. He sent other servants to say to the guests, "The banquet is ready! My cattle and prize calves have all been prepared. Everything is ready. Come to the banquet!"

But the guests did not pay any attention. Some of them left for their farms, and some went to their places of business. Others grabbed the servants, then beat them up and killed them.

This made the king so furious that he sent an army to kill those murderers and burn down their city. Then he said to the servants, "It is time for the wedding banquet, and the invited guests don't deserve to come. Go out to the street corners and tell everyone you meet to come to the banquet." They went out on the streets and brought in everyone they could find, good and bad alike. And the banquet room was filled with guests.

When the king went in to meet the guests, he found that one of them wasn't wearing the right kind of clothes for the wedding. The king asked, "Friend, why didn't you wear proper clothes for the wedding?" But the guest had no excuse. So the king gave orders for that person to be tied hand and foot and to be thrown outside into the dark. That's where people will cry and grit their teeth in pain. Many are invited, but only a few are chosen.

5.11 Paying Taxes to the Emperor

The Pharisees got together and planned how they could trick Jesus into saying something wrong. They sent some of their followers and some of Herod's followers to say to him, "Teacher, we know that you are honest. You teach the truth about what God wants people to do. And you treat everyone with the same respect, no matter who they are. Tell us what you think! Should we pay taxes to the Emperor or not?"

Jesus knew their evil thoughts and said, "Why are you trying to test me? You show-offs! Let me see one of the coins used for paying taxes." They brought him a silver coin, and he asked, "Whose picture and name are on it?"

"The Emperor's," they answered.

Then Jesus told them, "Give the Emperor what belongs to him and give God what belongs to God." His answer surprised them so much that they walked away.

5.12 Marriage and the Seven Brothers

The Sadducees did not believe that people would rise to life after death. So that same day some of the Sadducees came to Jesus and said:

> Teacher, Moses wrote that if a married man dies and has no children, his brother should marry the widow. Their first son would then be thought of as the son of the dead brother.
>
> Once there were seven brothers who lived here. The first one married, but died without having any children. So his wife was left to his brother. The same thing happened to the second and third brothers and finally to all seven of them. At last the woman died. When God raises people from death, whose wife will this woman be? She had been married to all seven brothers.

Jesus answered:

> You are completely wrong! You don't know what the Scriptures teach. And you don't know anything about the power of God. When God raises people to life, they won't marry. They will be like the angels in heaven. And as for people being raised to life, God was speaking to you when he said, "I am the God worshiped by Abraham, Isaac, and Jacob." He isn't the God of the dead, but of the living.

The crowds were surprised to hear what Jesus was teaching.

5.13 The Greatest Commandment

After Jesus had made the Sadducees look foolish, the Pharisees heard about it and got together. One of them was an expert in the Jewish Law. So he tried to test Jesus by asking, "Teacher, what is the most important commandment in the Law?"[129]

Jesus answered, "The most important one says: 'People of Israel, you have only one Lord and God. You must love him with all your heart, soul, mind, and strength.' The second most important commandment says: 'Love others as much as you love yourself.' No other commandment is more important than these."[130]

All the Law of Moses and the Books of the Prophets are based on these two commandments.[131] The man replied, "Teacher, you are certainly right to say there is only one God. It is also true that we must love God with all our heart, mind, and strength, and that we must love others as much as we love ourselves. These commandments are more important than all the sacrifices and offerings that we could possibly make."

When Jesus saw that the man had given a sensible answer, he told him, "You are not far from God's kingdom."[132]

5.14 Whose Son is the Messiah?

While the Pharisees were still there, Jesus asked them, "What do you think about the Messiah? Whose family will he come from?"

They answered, "He will be a son of King David."

Jesus replied, "How then could the Spirit have David call the Messiah his Lord? David said,

>'The Lord said to my Lord:
>   Sit at my right side
> until I make your enemies
>   into a footstool for you.'

If David called the Messiah his Lord, how can the Messiah be a son of King David?" No one was able to give Jesus an answer, and from that day on, no one dared ask him any more questions.

5.15 Jesus Accuses the Pharisees and the Teachers of the Law

Jesus said to the crowds and to his disciples:

The Pharisees and the teachers of the Law are experts in the Law of Moses. So obey everything they teach you, but don't do as they do. After all, they say one thing and do something else.

They pile heavy burdens on people's shoulders and won't lift a finger to help. Everything they do is just to show off in front of others. They even make a big show of wearing Scripture verses on their foreheads and arms, and they wear big tassels for everyone to see. They love the best seats at banquets and the front seats in the meeting places. And when they are in the market, they like to have people greet them as their teachers.

But none of you should be called a teacher. You have only one teacher, and all of you are like brothers and sisters. Don't call anyone on earth your father. All of you have the same Father in heaven. None of you should be called the leader. The Messiah is your only leader.

Whoever is the greatest should be the servant of the others. If you put yourself above others, you will be put down. But if you humble yourself, you will be honored.

You Pharisees and teachers of the Law of Moses are in for trouble! You're nothing but show-offs. You lock people out of the kingdom of heaven. You won't go in yourselves, and you keep others from going in.

You Pharisees and teachers of the Law of Moses are in for trouble! You're nothing but show-offs. You travel over land and sea to win one follower. And when you have done so, you make that person twice as fit for hell as you are.

You are in for trouble! You are supposed to lead others, but you are blind. You teach that it doesn't matter if a person swears by the temple. But you say that it does matter if someone swears by the gold in the temple. You blind fools! Which is greater, the gold or the temple that makes the gold sacred?

You also teach that it doesn't matter if a person swears by the altar. But you say that it does matter if someone swears by the gift on the altar. Are you blind? Which is more important, the gift or the altar that makes the gift sacred? Anyone who swears by the altar also swears by everything on it. And anyone who swears by the temple also swears by God, who lives there. To swear by heaven is the same as swearing by God's throne and by the one who sits on that throne.

You Pharisees and teachers are show-offs, and you're in for trouble! You give God a tenth of the spices from your garden, such as mint, dill, and cumin. Yet you neglect the more important matters of the Law, such as justice, mercy, and faithfulness. These are the important things you should have done, though you should not have left the others undone either. You blind leaders! You strain out a small fly but swallow a camel.

You Pharisees and teachers are show-offs, and you're in for trouble! You wash the outside of your cups and dishes, while inside there is nothing but greed and selfishness. You blind Pharisee! First clean the inside of a cup, and then the outside will also be clean.

You Pharisees and teachers are in for trouble! You're nothing but show-offs. You're like tombs that have been whitewashed. On the outside they are beautiful, but inside they are full of bones and filth. That's what you are like. Outside you look good, but inside you are evil and only pretend to be good.

You Pharisees and teachers are nothing but show-offs, and you're in for trouble! You build monuments for the prophets and decorate the tombs of good people. And you claim that you would not have taken part with your ancestors in killing the prophets. But you prove that you really are the relatives of the ones who killed the prophets. So keep on doing everything they did. You are nothing but snakes and the children of snakes! How can you escape going to hell?

I will send prophets and wise people and experts in the Law of Moses to you. But you will kill them or nail them to a cross or beat them in your meeting places or chase them from town to town. That's why you will be held guilty for the murder of every good person, beginning with the good man Abel. This also includes Barachiah's son Zechariah, the man you murdered between the temple and the altar. I can promise that you people living today will be punished for all these things!

Jerusalem, Jerusalem! Your people have killed the prophets and have stoned the messengers who were sent to you. I have often wanted to gather your people, as a hen gathers her chicks under her wings. But you wouldn't let me. And now your temple will be deserted. You won't see me again until you say,

"Blessed is the one who comes
in the name of the Lord." [133]

5.16 The Widow's Offering

Jesus was sitting in the temple near the offering box and watching people put in their gifts. He noticed that many rich people were giving a lot of money. Finally, a poor widow came up and put in two coins that were worth only a few pennies. Jesus told his disciples to gather around him. Then he said:

I tell you that this poor widow has put in more than all the others. Everyone else gave what they didn't need. But she is very poor and gave everything she had. Now she doesn't have a cent to live on.

5.17 Signs of the End of the Age

As Jesus was leaving the temple, one of his disciples said to him, "Teacher, look at these beautiful stones and wonderful buildings!"

Jesus replied, "Do you see these huge buildings? They will certainly be torn down! Not one stone will be left in place."

Later, as Jesus was sitting on the Mount of Olives across from the temple, Peter, James, John, and Andrew came to him in private. They asked,

"When will these things happen? What will be the sign that they are about to take place?"

Jesus answered:

Watch out and don't let anyone fool you! Many will come and claim to be me. They will use my name and fool many people.

When you hear about wars and threats of wars, don't be afraid. These things will have to happen first, but that isn't the end. Nations and kingdoms will go to war against each other. There will be earthquakes in many places, and people will starve to death. But this is just the beginning of troubles.

Be on your guard! You will be taken to courts and beaten with whips in their meeting places. And because of me, you will have to stand before rulers and kings to tell about your faith. But before the end comes, the good news must be preached to all nations.

When you are arrested, don't worry about what you will say. You will be given the right words when the time comes. But you will not really be the ones speaking. Your words will come from the Holy Spirit.

Brothers and sisters will betray each other and have each other put to death. Parents will betray their own children, and children will turn against their parents and have them killed. Everyone will hate you because of me. But if you keep on being faithful right to the end, you will be saved. [134]

Many false prophets will come and fool a lot of people. Evil will spread and cause many people to stop loving others. But if you keep on being faithful right to the end, you will be saved. When the good news about the kingdom has been preached all over the world and told to all nations, the end will come.

Someday you will see that "Horrible Thing" in the holy place, just as the prophet Daniel said. Everyone who reads this must try to understand! If you are living in Judea at that time, run to the mountains. If you are on the roof of your house, don't go inside to get anything. If you are out in the field, don't go back for your coat. It will be a terrible time for women who are expecting babies or nursing young children. And pray that you won't have to escape in winter or on a Sabbath. This will be the worst time of suffering since the beginning of the world, and nothing this terrible will ever happen again. If God doesn't make the time shorter, no one will be left alive. But because of God's chosen ones, he will make the time shorter.

Someone may say, "Here is the Messiah!" or "There he is!" But don't believe it. False messiahs and false prophets will come and work great miracles and signs. They will even try to fool God's chosen ones. But I have warned you ahead of time. If you are told that the Messiah is out in the desert, don't go there! And if you are told that he is in some secret place, don't believe it! The coming of the Son of Man will be like lightning that can be seen from east to west. Where there is a corpse, there will always be buzzards.

Right after those days of suffering,

"The sun will become dark,
    and the moon will no longer shine.
The stars will fall,
    and the powers in the sky will be shaken."

Then a sign will appear in the sky. And there will be the Son of Man. All nations on earth will weep when they see the Son of Man coming on the clouds of heaven with power and great glory. At the sound of a loud trumpet, he will send his angels to bring his chosen ones together from all over the earth.[135]

When all of this starts happening, stand up straight and be brave. You will soon be set free.

Then Jesus told them a story:

When you see a fig tree or any other tree putting out leaves, you know that summer will soon come. So, when you see these things happening, you know that God's kingdom will soon be here. You can be sure that some of the people of this generation will still be alive when all of this takes place. The sky and the earth won't last forever, but my words will.[136]

5.18 The Day and Hour Unknown

No one knows the day or hour. The angels in heaven don't know, and the Son himself doesn't know. Only the Father knows. When the Son of Man appears, things will be just as they were when Noah lived. People were eating, drinking, and getting married right up to the day that the flood came and Noah went into the big boat. They didn't know anything was happening until the flood came and swept them all away. That is how it will be when the Son of Man appears.

Two men will be in the same field, but only one will be taken. The other will be left. Two women will be together grinding grain, but only one will be taken. The other will be left.[137]

Don't spend all of your time thinking about eating or drinking or worrying about life. If you do, the final day will suddenly catch you like a trap. That day will surprise everyone on earth. Watch out and keep praying that you can escape all that is going to happen and that the Son of Man will be pleased with you.[138]

It is like what happens when a man goes away for a while and places his servants in charge of everything. He tells each of them what to do, and he orders the guard to keep alert. So be alert! You don't know when the master of the house will come back. It could be in the evening or at midnight or before dawn or in the morning. But if he comes suddenly, don't let him find you asleep. I tell everyone just what I have told you. Be alert![139]

Homeowners never know when a thief is coming, and they are always on guard to keep one from breaking in. Always be ready! You don't know when the Son of Man will come.

Who are faithful and wise servants? Who are the ones the master will put in charge of giving the other servants their food supplies at the proper time? Servants are fortunate if their master comes and finds them doing their job. You may be sure that a servant who is always faithful will be put in charge of everything the master owns. But suppose one of the servants thinks that the master won't return until late. Suppose that evil servant starts beating the other servants and eats and drinks with people who are drunk. If that happens, the master will surely come on a day and at a time when the servant least expects him. That servant will then be punished and thrown out with the ones who only pretended to serve their master. There they will cry and grit their teeth in pain.

5.19 The Parable of the Ten Girls

The kingdom of heaven is like what happened one night when ten girls took their oil lamps and went to a wedding to meet the groom. Five of the girls were foolish and five were wise. The foolish ones took their lamps, but no extra oil. The ones who were wise took along extra oil for their lamps.

The groom was late arriving, and the girls became drowsy and fell asleep. Then in the middle of the night someone shouted, "Here's the groom! Come to meet him!"

When the girls got up and started getting their lamps ready, the foolish ones said to the others, "Let us have some of your oil! Our lamps are going out."

The girls who were wise answered, "There's not enough oil for all of us! Go and buy some for yourselves."

While the foolish girls were on their way to get some oil, the groom arrived. The girls who were ready went into the wedding, and the doors were closed. Later the other girls returned and shouted, "Sir, sir! Open the door for us!"

But the groom replied, "I don't even know you!"

So, my disciples, always be ready! You don't know the day or the time when all this will happen.

5.20 The Parable of the Coins

The kingdom is also like what happened when a man went away and put his three servants in charge of all he owned. The man knew what each servant could do. So he handed five thousand coins to the first servant, two thousand to the second, and one thousand to the third. Then he left the country.

As soon as the man had gone, the servant with the five thousand coins used them to earn five thousand more. The servant who had two thousand coins did the same with his money and earned two thousand more. But the servant with one thousand coins dug a hole and hid his master's money in the ground.

Some time later the master of those servants returned. He called them in and asked what they had done with his money. The servant who had been given five thousand coins brought them in with the five thousand that he had earned. He said, "Sir, you gave me five thousand coins, and I have earned five thousand more."

"Wonderful!" his master replied. "You are a good and faithful servant. I left you in charge of only a little, but now I will put you in charge of much more. Come and share in my happiness!"

Next, the servant who had been given two thousand coins came in and said, "Sir, you gave me two thousand coins, and I have earned two thousand more."

"Wonderful!" his master replied. "You are a good and faithful servant. I left you in charge of only a little, but now I will put you in charge of much more. Come and share in my happiness!"

The servant who had been given one thousand coins then came in and said, "Sir, I know that you are hard to get along with. You harvest what you don't plant and gather crops where you haven't scattered seed. I was frightened and went out and hid your money in the ground. Here is every single coin!"

The master of the servant told him, "You are lazy and good-for-nothing! You know that I harvest what I don't plant and gather crops where I haven't scattered seed. You could have at least put my money in the bank, so that I could have earned interest on it".

Then the master said, "Now your money will be taken away and given to the servant with ten thousand coins! Everyone who has something will be given more, and they will have more than enough. But everything will be taken from those who don't have anything. You are a worthless servant, and you will be thrown out into the dark where people will cry and grit their teeth in pain."

5.21 The Sheep and the Goats

When the Son of Man comes in his glory with all of his angels, he will sit on his royal throne. The people of all nations will be brought before him, and he will separate them, as shepherds separate their sheep from their goats.

He will place the sheep on his right and the goats on his left. Then the king will say to those on his right, "My father has blessed you! Come and receive the kingdom that was prepared for you before the world was created. When I was hungry, you gave me something to eat, and when I was thirsty, you gave me something to drink. When I was a stranger, you welcomed me, and when I was naked, you gave me clothes to wear. When I was sick, you took care of me, and when I was in jail, you visited me."

Then the ones who pleased the Lord will ask, When did we give you something to eat or drink? When did we welcome you as a stranger or give you clothes to wear or visit you while you were sick or in jail?

The king will answer, "Whenever you did it for any of my people, no matter how unimportant they seemed, you did it for me."

Then the king will say to those on his left, "Get away from me! You are under God's curse. Go into the everlasting fire prepared for the devil and his angels! I was hungry, but you did not give me anything to eat, and I was thirsty, but you did not give me anything to drink. I was a stranger, but you did not welcome me, and I was naked, but you did not give me any clothes to wear. I was sick and in jail, but you did not take care of me."

Then the people will ask, "Lord, when did we fail to help you when you were hungry or thirsty or a stranger or naked or sick or in jail?"

The king will say to them, "Whenever you failed to help any of my people, no matter how unimportant they seemed, you failed to do it for me."

Then Jesus said, "Those people will be punished forever. But the ones who pleased God will have eternal life."

5.22 The Plot Against Jesus

When Jesus had finished teaching, he told his disciples, "You know that two days from now will be Passover. That is when the Son of Man will be handed over to his enemies and nailed to a cross."

At that time the chief priests and the nation's leaders were meeting at the home of Caiaphas the high priest. They planned how they could sneak around and have Jesus arrested and put to death. But they said, "We must not do it during Passover, because the people will riot." [140]

5.23 Judas Agrees to Betray Jesus

Then Satan entered the heart of Judas Iscariot, who was one of the twelve apostles.

Judas went to talk with the chief priests and the officers of the temple police about how he could help them arrest Jesus, [141] and asked, "How much will you give me if I help you arrest Jesus?" They paid Judas thirty silver coins, and from then on he started looking for a good chance to betray Jesus.[142]

5.24 Preparations for the Last Supper

The day had come for the Festival of Thin Bread, and it was time to kill the Passover lambs. So Jesus said to Peter and John, "Go and prepare the Passover meal for us to eat."

But they asked, "Where do you want us to prepare it?"

Jesus told them, "As you go into the city, you will meet a man carrying a jar of water. Follow him into the house and say to the owner, 'Our teacher wants to know where he can eat the Passover meal with his disciples.' The owner will take you upstairs and show you a large room ready for you to use. Prepare the meal there."

Peter and John left. They found everything just as Jesus had told them, and they prepared the Passover meal.

The Lord's Supper (5.25-40)

5.25 Who is the Greatest?

When the time came for Jesus and the apostles to eat, [143] the apostles got into an argument about which one of them was the greatest. So Jesus told them:

Foreign kings order their people around, and powerful rulers call themselves everyone's friends. But don't be like them. The most important one of you should be like the least important, and your leader should be like a servant. Who do people think is the greatest, a person who is served or one who serves? Isn't it the one who is served? But I have been with you as a servant.

You have stayed with me in all my troubles. So I will give you the right to rule as kings, just as my Father has given me the right to rule as a king. You will eat and drink with me in my kingdom, and you will each sit on a throne to judge the twelve tribes of Israel.[144]

5.26 Jesus Washes His Disciples' Feet

Jesus knew that he had come from God and would go back to God. He also knew that the Father had given him complete power. So during the meal Jesus got up, removed his outer garment, and wrapped a towel around his waist. He put some water into a large bowl. Then he began washing his disciples' feet and drying them with the towel he was wearing.

But when he came to Simon Peter, that disciple asked, "Lord, are you going to wash my feet?"

Jesus answered, "You don't really know what I am doing, but later you will understand."

"You will never wash my feet!" Peter replied.

"If I don't wash you," Jesus told him, "you don't really belong to me."

Peter said, "Lord, don't wash just my feet. Wash my hands and my head."

Jesus answered, "People who have bathed and are clean all over need to wash just their feet. And you, my disciples, are clean, except for one of you." Jesus knew who would betray him. That is why he said, "except for one of you."

After Jesus had washed his disciples' feet and had put his outer garment back on, he sat down again. Then he said:

> Do you understand what I have done? You call me your teacher and Lord, and you should, because that is who I am. And if your Lord and teacher has washed your feet, you should do the same for each other. I have set the example, and you should do for each other exactly what I have done for you. I tell you for certain that servants are not greater than their master, and messengers are not greater than the one who sent them. You know these things, and God will bless you, if you do them.

5.27 Jesus Predicts Judas' Betrayal

I am not talking about all of you. I know the ones I have chosen. But what the Scriptures say must come true. And they say, "The man who ate with me has turned against me!" I am telling you this before it all happens. Then when it does happen, you will believe who I am. I tell you for certain that anyone who welcomes my messengers also welcomes me, and anyone who welcomes me welcomes the one who sent me. [145]

He said to them, "I have very much wanted to eat this Passover meal with you before I suffer. I tell you that I will not eat another Passover meal until it is finally eaten in God's kingdom."[146]

When Jesus was eating with his twelve disciples that evening, he said, "One of you will surely hand me over to my enemies."[147]

They were confused about what he meant. And they just stared at each other.[148]

The disciples were very sad, and each one said to Jesus, "Lord, you can't mean me!"[149]

Jesus' favorite disciple was sitting next to him at the meal, and Simon motioned for that disciple to find out which one Jesus meant. So the disciple leaned toward Jesus and asked, "Lord, which one of us are you talking about?"

Jesus answered, "I will dip this piece of bread in the sauce and give it to the one I was talking about.[150]

The Son of Man will die, as the Scriptures say. But it's going to be terrible for the one who betrays me! That man would be better off if he had never been born."

Judas said, "Teacher, you surely don't mean me!"

"That's what you say!" Jesus replied. But later, Judas did betray him.[151]

Then Jesus dipped the bread and gave it to Judas, the son of Simon Iscariot. Right then Satan took control of Judas.

Jesus said, "Judas, go quickly and do what you have to do." No one at the meal understood what Jesus meant. But because Judas was in charge of the money, some of them thought that Jesus had told him to buy something they needed for the festival. Others thought that Jesus had told him to give some money to the poor. Judas took the piece of bread and went out.

It was already night.[152]

5.28 The Lord's Supper

Jesus took a cup of wine in his hands and gave thanks to God. Then he told the apostles, "Take this wine and share it with each other. I tell you that I will not drink any more wine until God's kingdom comes."[153]

During the meal Jesus took some bread in his hands. He blessed the bread and broke it. Then he gave it to his disciples and said, "Take this and eat it. This is my body [154] given for you. Eat this as a way of remembering me!"

After the meal he took another cup of wine in his hands,[155] and gave thanks to God. He then gave it to his disciples and said, "Take this and drink it.[156] This is my blood. It is poured out for you, and with it God makes his new agreement. [157] It will be poured out, so that many people will have their sins forgiven. From now on I am not going to drink any wine, until I drink new wine with you in my Father's kingdom."[158]

5.29 A New Command

After Judas had gone, Jesus said:

Now the Son of Man will be given glory, and he will bring glory to God. Then, after God is given glory because of him, God will bring glory to him, and God will do it very soon.

My children, I will be with you for a little while longer. Then you will look for me, but you won't find me. I tell you just as I told the people, "You cannot go where I am going." But I am giving you a new command. You must love each other, just as I have loved you. If you love each other, everyone will know that you are my disciples.

5.30 Jesus Predicts Peter's Denial

Simon Peter asked, "Lord, where are you going?"

Jesus answered, "You can't go with me now, but later on you will."

Peter asked, "Lord, why can't I go with you now? I would die for you!"[159]

Jesus said to his disciples, "During this very night, all of you will reject me, as the Scriptures say,

'I will strike down the shepherd,
    and the sheep will be scattered.'

But after I am raised to life, I will go to Galilee ahead of you."

Peter spoke up, "Even if all the others reject you, I never will!"[160]

Jesus said, "Simon, listen to me! Satan has demanded the right to test each one of you, as a farmer does when he separates wheat from the husks. But Simon, I have prayed that your faith will be strong. And when you have come back to me, help the others."

Peter said, "Lord, I am ready to go with you to jail and even to die with you."[161]

"Would you really die for me?" Jesus asked. "I tell you for certain,[162] this very night before a rooster crows twice, you will say three times that you don't know me."

But Peter was so sure of himself that he said, "Even if I have to die with you, I will never say that I don't know you!"

All the others said the same thing. [163]

Jesus asked his disciples, "When I sent you out without a moneybag or a traveling bag or sandals, did you need anything?"

"No!" they answered.

Jesus told them, "But now, if you have a moneybag, take it with you. Also take a traveling bag, and if you don't have a sword, sell some of your clothes and buy one. Do this because the Scriptures say, 'He was considered a criminal.' This was written about me, and it will soon come true."

The disciples said, "Lord, here are two swords!"

"Enough of that!" Jesus replied. [164]

5.31 Jesus Comforts His Disciples

Jesus said to his disciples, "Don't be worried! Have faith in God and have faith in me. There are many rooms in my Father's house. I wouldn't tell you this, unless it was true. I am going there to prepare a place for each of you. After I have done this, I will come back and take you with me. Then we will be together. You know the way to where I am going."

5.32 Jesus Is the Way to the Father

Thomas said, "Lord, we don't even know where you are going! How can we know the way?"

"I am the way, the truth, and the life!" Jesus answered. "Without me, no one can go to the Father. If you had known me, you would have known the Father. But from now on, you do know him, and you have seen him."

Philip said, "Lord, show us the Father. That is all we need."

Jesus replied:

Philip, I have been with you for a long time. Don't you know who I am? If you have seen me, you have seen the Father. How can you ask me to show you the Father? Don't you believe that I am one with the Father and that the Father is one with me? What I say isn't said on my own. The Father who lives in me does these things.

Have faith in me when I say that the Father is one with me and that I am one with the Father. Or else have faith in me simply because of the things I do. I tell you for certain that if you have faith in me, you will do the same things that I am doing. You will do even greater things, now that I am going back to the Father. Ask me, and I will do whatever you ask. This way the Son will bring honor to the Father. I will do whatever you ask me to do.

5.33 Jesus Promises the Holy Spirit

Jesus said to his disciples:

If you love me, you will do as I command. Then I will ask the Father to send you the Holy Spirit who will help you and always be with you. The Spirit will show you what is true. The people of this world cannot accept the Spirit, because they don't see or know him. But you know the Spirit, who is with you and will keep on living in you.

I won't leave you like orphans. I will come back to you. In a little while the people of this world won't be able to see me, but you will see me. And because I live, you will live. Then you will know that I am one with the Father. You will know that you are one with me, and I am one with you. If you love me, you will do what I have said, and my Father will love you. I will also love you and show you what I am like.

The other Judas, not Judas Iscariot, then spoke up and asked, "Lord, what do you mean by saying that you will show us what you are like, but you will not show the people of this world?"

Jesus replied:

If anyone loves me, they will obey me. Then my Father will love them, and we will come to them and live in them. But anyone who doesn't love me, won't obey me. What they have heard me say doesn't really come from me, but from the Father who sent me.

I have told you these things while I am still with you. But the Holy Spirit will come and help you, because the Father will send the Spirit to take my place. The Spirit will teach you everything and will remind you of what I said while I was with you.

I give you peace, the kind of peace that only I can give. It isn't like the peace that this world can give. So don't be worried or afraid.

You have already heard me say that I am going and that I will also come back to you. If you really love me, you should be glad that I am going back to the Father, because he is greater than I am.

I am telling you this before I leave, so that when it does happen, you will have faith in me. I cannot speak with you much longer, because the ruler of this world is coming. But he has no power over me. I obey my Father, so that everyone in the world might know that I love him.

It is time for us to go now.

5.34 The Vine and the Branches

Jesus said to his disciples:

I am the true vine, and my Father is the gardener. He cuts away every branch of mine that doesn't produce fruit. But he trims clean every branch that does produce fruit, so that it will produce even more fruit. You are already clean because of what I have said to you.

Stay joined to me, and I will stay joined to you. Just as a branch cannot produce fruit unless it stays joined to the vine, you cannot produce fruit unless you stay joined to me. I am the vine, and you are the branches. If you stay joined to me, and I stay joined to you, then you will produce lots of fruit. But you cannot do anything without me. If you don't stay joined to me, you will be thrown away. You will be like dry branches that are gathered up and burned in a fire.

Stay joined to me and let my teachings become part of you. Then you can pray for whatever you want, and your prayer will be answered. When you become fruitful disciples of mine, my Father will be honored. I have loved you, just as my Father has loved me. So remain faithful to my love for you. If you obey me, I will keep loving you, just as my Father keeps loving me, because I have obeyed him.

I have told you this to make you as completely happy as I am. Now I tell you to love each other, as I have loved you. The greatest way to show love for friends is to die for them. And you are my friends, if you obey me. Servants don't know what their master is doing, and so I don't speak to you as my servants. I speak to you as my friends, and I have told you everything that my Father has told me.

You did not choose me. I chose you and sent you out to produce fruit, the kind of fruit that will last. Then my Father will give you whatever you ask for in my name. So I command you to love each other.

5.35 The World Hates the Disciples

If the people of this world hate you, just remember that they hated me first. If you belonged to the world, its people would love you. But you don't belong to the world. I have chosen you to leave the world behind, and that is why its people hate you. Remember how I told you that servants are not greater than their master. So if people mistreat me, they will mistreat you. If they do what I say, they will do what you say.

People will do to you exactly what they did to me. They will do it because you belong to me, and they don't know the one who sent me. If I had not come and spoken to them, they would not be guilty of sin. But now they have no excuse for their sin.

Everyone who hates me also hates my Father. I have done things that no one else has ever done. If they had not seen me do these things, they would not be guilty. But they did see me do these things, and they still hate me and my Father too. That is why the Scriptures are true when they say, "People hated me for no reason."

I will send you the Spirit who comes from the Father and shows what is true. The Spirit will help you and will tell you about me. Then you will also tell others about me, because you have been with me from the beginning.

I am telling you this to keep you from being afraid. You will be chased out of the Jewish meeting places. And the time will come when people will kill you and think they are doing God a favor. They will do these things because they don't know either the Father or me. I am saying this to you now, so that when the time comes, you will remember what I have said.

5.36 The Work of the Holy Spirit

I was with you at the first, and so I didn't tell you these things. But now I am going back to the Father who sent me, and none of you asks me where I am going. You are very sad from hearing all of this. But I tell you that I am going to do what is best for you. That is why I am going away. The Holy Spirit cannot come to help you until I leave. But after I am gone, I will send the Spirit to you.

The Spirit will come and show the people of this world the truth about sin and God's justice and the judgment. The Spirit will show them that they are wrong about sin, because they didn't have faith in me. They are wrong about God's justice, because I am going to the Father, and you won't see me again. And they are wrong about the judgment, because God has already judged the ruler of this world.

I have much more to say to you, but right now it would be more than you could understand. The Spirit shows what is true and will come and guide you into the full truth. The Spirit doesn't speak on his own. He will tell you only what he has heard from me, and he will let you know what is going to happen. The Spirit will bring glory to me by taking my message and telling it to you. Everything that the Father has is mine. That is why I have said that the Spirit takes my message and tells it to you.

5.37 The Disciples Grief Will Turn to Joy

Jesus told his disciples, "For a little while you won't see me, but after a while you will see me."

They said to each other, "What does Jesus mean by saying that for a little while we won't see him, but after a while we will see him? What does he mean by saying that he is going to the Father? What is this 'little while' that he is talking about? We don't know what he means."

Jesus knew that they had some questions, so he said:

> You are wondering what I meant when I said that for a little while you won't see me, but after a while you will see me. I tell you for certain that you will cry and be sad, but the world will be happy. You will be sad, but later you will be happy.
>
> When a woman is about to give birth, she is in great pain. But after it is all over, she forgets the pain and is happy, because she has brought a child into the world. You are now very sad. But later I will see you, and you will be so happy that no one will be able to change the way you feel. When that time comes, you won't have to ask me about anything. I tell you for certain that the Father will give you whatever you ask for in my name. You have not asked for anything in this way before, but now you must ask in my name. Then it will be given to you, so that you will be completely happy.
>
> I have used examples to explain to you what I have been talking about. But the time will come when I will speak to you plainly about the Father and will no longer use examples like these. You will ask the Father in my name, and I won't have to ask him for you. God the Father loves you because you love me, and you believe that I have come from him. I came from the Father into the world, but I am leaving the world and returning to the Father.

The disciples said, "Now you are speaking plainly to us! You are not using examples. At last we know that you understand everything, and we don't have any more questions. Now we believe that you truly have come from God."

Jesus replied:

> Do you really believe me? The time will come and is already

here when all of you will be scattered. Each of you will go back home and leave me by myself. But the Father will be with me, and I won't be alone. I have told you this, so that you might have peace in your hearts because of me. While you are in the world, you will have to suffer. But cheer up! I have defeated the world.

5.38 Jesus Prays for Himself

After Jesus had finished speaking to his disciples, he looked up toward heaven and prayed:

Father, the time has come for you to bring glory to your Son, in order that he may bring glory to you. And you gave him power over all people, so that he would give eternal life to everyone you give him. Eternal life is to know you, the only true God, and to know Jesus Christ, the one you sent. I have brought glory to you here on earth by doing everything you gave me to do. Now, Father, give me back the glory that I had with you before the world was created.

5.39 Jesus Prays for His Disciples

You have given me some followers from this world, and I have shown them what you are like. They were yours, but you gave them to me, and they have obeyed you. They know that you gave me everything I have. I told my followers what you told me, and they accepted it. They know that I came from you, and they believe that you are the one who sent me. I am praying for them, but not for those who belong to this world. My followers belong to you, and I am praying for them. All that I have is yours, and all that you have is mine, and they will bring glory to me.

Holy Father, I am no longer in the world. I am coming to you, but my followers are still in the world. So keep them safe by the power of the name that you have given me. Then they will be one with each other, just as you and I are one. While I was with them, I kept them safe by the power you have given me. I guarded them, and not one of them was lost, except the one who had to be lost. This happened so that what the Scriptures say would come true.

I am on my way to you. But I say these things while I am still in the world, so that my followers will have the same complete joy that I do. I have told them your message. But the people of this world hate them, because they don't belong to this world, just as I don't.

Father, I don't ask you to take my followers out of the world, but keep them safe from the evil one. They don't belong to this world, and neither do I. Your word is the truth. So let this truth make them completely yours. I am sending them into the world, just as you sent me. I have given myself completely for their sake, so that they may belong completely to the truth.

5.40 Jesus Prays for All Believers

I am not praying just for these followers. I am also praying for everyone else who will have faith because of what my followers will say about me. I want all of them to be one with each other, just as I am one with you and you are one with me. I also want them to be one with us. Then the people of this world will believe that you sent me.

I have honored my followers in the same way that you honored me, in order that they may be one with each other, just as we are one. I am one with them, and you are one with me, so that they may become completely one. Then this world's people will know that you sent me. They will know that you love my followers as much as you love me.

Father, I want everyone you have given me to be with me, wherever I am. Then they will see the glory that you have given me, because you loved me before the world was created. Good Father, the people of this world don't know you. But I know you, and my followers know that you sent me. I told them what you are like, and I will tell them even more. Then the love that you have for me will become part of them, and I will be one with them. [165]

5.41 Gethsemane

Then they sang a hymn and went out to the Mount of Olives. [166]

Jesus went with his disciples to a place called Gethsemane. When they got there, he told them, "Sit here while I go over there and pray."

Jesus took along Peter and the two brothers, James and John. He was very sad and troubled, and he said to them, "I am so sad that I feel as if I am dying. Stay here and keep awake with me."

Jesus walked on a little way. Then he knelt with his face to the ground and prayed, "My Father, if it is possible, don't make me suffer by having me drink from this cup. But do what you want, and not what I want." [167]

Then an angel from heaven came to help him. Jesus was in great pain and prayed so sincerely that his sweat fell to the ground like drops of blood. [168]

He came back and found his disciples sleeping. So he said to Peter, "Can't any of you stay awake with me for just one hour? Stay awake and pray that you won't be tested. You want to do what is right, but you are weak."

Again Jesus went to pray and said, "My Father, if there is no other way, and I must suffer, I will still do what you want."

Jesus came back and found them sleeping again. They simply could not keep their eyes open. He left them and prayed the same prayer once more.

Finally, Jesus returned to his disciples and said, "Are you still sleeping and resting? The time has come for the Son of Man to be handed over to sinners. Get up! Let's go. The one who will betray me is already here." [169]

5.42 Jesus Arrested

Jesus had often met there with his disciples, and Judas knew where the place was.

Judas had promised to betray Jesus. So he went to the garden with some Roman soldiers and temple police, who had been sent by the chief priests and the Pharisees. They carried torches, lanterns, and weapons. Jesus already knew everything that was going to happen, but he asked, "Who are you looking for?"

They answered, "We are looking for Jesus from Nazareth!"

Jesus told them, "I am Jesus!" At once they all backed away and fell to the ground.

Jesus again asked, "Who are you looking for?"

"We are looking for Jesus from Nazareth," they answered.

This time Jesus replied, "I have already told you that I am Jesus. If I am the one you are looking for, let these others go. Then everything will happen, just as I said, 'I did not lose anyone you gave me.'" [170]

Judas had told them ahead of time, "Arrest the man I greet with a kiss."

Judas walked right up to Jesus and said, "Hello, teacher." Then Judas kissed him. [171]

Jesus asked Judas, "Are you betraying the Son of Man with a kiss?"[172] And the men grabbed Jesus and arrested him. [173]

Simon Peter had brought along a sword. He now pulled it out and struck at the servant of the high priest. The servant's name was Malchus, and Peter cut off his right ear. [174]

"Enough of that!" Jesus said. Then he touched the servant's ear and healed it. [175]

Jesus told Peter, "Put your sword away. [176] Anyone who lives by fighting will die by fighting.[177] I must drink from the cup that the Father has given me.[178]

Don't you know that I could ask my Father, and right away he would send me more than twelve armies of angels? But then, how could the words of the Scriptures come true, which say that this must happen?"

Jesus said to the mob, "Why do you come with swords and clubs to arrest me like a criminal? Day after day I sat and taught in the temple, and you didn't arrest me. But all this happened, so that what the prophets wrote would come true."

All of Jesus' disciples left him and ran away.[179] One of them was a young man who was wearing only a linen cloth. And when the men grabbed him, he left the cloth behind and ran away naked.[180]

Jesus Taken to Annas

The Roman officer and his men, together with the temple police, arrested Jesus and tied him up. They took him first to Annas, who was the father-in-law of Caiaphas, the high priest that year. This was the same Caiaphas who had told the Jewish leaders, "It is better if one person dies for the people."[181] Jesus was still tied up, and Annas sent him to Caiaphas the high priest.[182]

After Jesus had been arrested, he was led off to the house of Caiaphas the high priest. The nation's leaders and the teachers of the Law of Moses were meeting there.[183]

Peter's First Denial

Simon Peter and another disciple followed Jesus. That disciple knew the high priest, and he followed Jesus into the courtyard of the high priest's house. Peter stayed outside near the gate. But the other disciple came back out and spoke to the girl at the gate. She let Peter go in. [184]

It was cold, and the servants and temple police had made a charcoal fire. They were warming themselves around it, when Peter went over and stood near the fire to warm himself. [185]

While Peter was still in the courtyard, a servant girl of the high priest came up and saw Peter warming himself by the fire. [186] She asked him, "Aren't you one of that man's followers?"[187] She stared at him and said, "You were with Jesus from Nazareth!"

Peter replied, "That isn't true! I don't know what you're talking about. I don't have any idea what you mean." He went out to the gate, and a rooster crowed. [188]

5.45 The High Priest Questions Jesus

The high priest questioned Jesus about his followers and his teaching. But Jesus told him, "I have spoken freely in front of everyone. And I have always taught in our meeting places and in the temple, where all of our people come together. I have not said anything in secret. Why are you questioning me? Why don't you ask the people who heard me? They know what I have said."

As soon as Jesus said this, one of the temple police hit him and said, "That's no way to talk to the high priest!"

Jesus answered, "If I have done something wrong, say so. But if not, why did you hit me?" [189]

5.46 Peter's Second and Third Denials

While Simon Peter was standing there warming himself, someone asked him, "Aren't you one of Jesus' followers?" [190]

The servant girl saw Peter again and said to the people standing there, "This man is one of them!"

"No, I'm not!" Peter replied.

A little while later some of the people said to Peter, "You certainly are one of them. You're a Galilean!" [191]

One of the high priest's servants was there. He was a relative of the servant whose ear Peter had cut off, and he asked, "Didn't I see you in the garden with that man?" [192]

This time Peter began to curse and swear, "I don't even know the man you're talking about!" [193]

Right then, while Peter was still speaking, a rooster crowed.

The Lord turned and looked at Peter. And Peter remembered that the Lord had said, "Before a rooster crows tomorrow morning, you will say three times that you don't know me." Then Peter went out and cried hard. [194]

5.47 Jesus Before the Whole Council

The chief priests and the whole council tried to find someone to accuse Jesus of a crime, so they could put him to death. But they could not find anyone to accuse him. Many people did tell lies against Jesus, but they did not agree on what they said. [195]

At last, two men came forward and said, "This man claimed that he would tear down God's temple and build it again in three days." [196]

"We heard him say he would tear down this temple that we built. He also claimed that in three days he would build another one without any help." But even then they did not agree on what they said.

The high priest stood up in the council and asked Jesus, "Why don't you say something in your own defense? Don't you hear the charges they are making against you?" But Jesus kept quiet and did not say a word. The high priest asked him another question, "Are you the Messiah, the Son of the glorious God?"

"Yes, I am!" Jesus answered.

"Soon you will see the Son of Man
sitting at the right side of God All-Powerful,
    and coming with the clouds of heaven."

At once the high priest ripped his robe apart and shouted, "Why do we need more witnesses? You heard him claim to be God! What is your decision?" They all agreed that he should be put to death.

Some of the people started spitting on Jesus. They blindfolded him, hit him with their fists, and said, "Tell us who hit you!" Then the guards took charge of Jesus and beat him. [197]

At daybreak the nation's leaders, the chief priests, and the teachers of the Law of Moses got together and brought Jesus before their council. They said, "Tell us! Are you the Messiah?"

Jesus replied, "If I said so, you wouldn't believe me. And if I asked you a question, you wouldn't answer. But from now on, the Son of Man will be seated at the right side of God All-Powerful."

Then they asked, "Are you the Son of God?"

Jesus answered, "You say I am!"

They replied, "Why do we need more witnesses? He said it himself!" [198]

5.48 Judas Hangs Himself

Early the next morning all the chief priests and the nation's leaders met and decided that Jesus should be put to death. They tied him up and led him away to Pilate the governor.

Judas had betrayed Jesus, but when he learned that Jesus had been sentenced to death, he was sorry for what he had done. He returned the thirty silver coins to the chief priests and leaders and said, "I have sinned by betraying a man who has never done anything wrong."

"So what? That's your problem," they replied. Judas threw the money into the temple and then went out and hanged himself.

The chief priests picked up the money and said, "This money was paid to have a man killed. We can't put it in the temple treasury." Then they had a meeting and decided to buy a field that belonged to someone who made clay pots. They wanted to use it as a graveyard for foreigners. That's why people still call that place "Field of Blood." So the words of the prophet Jeremiah came true,

> "They took the thirty silver coins,
>   the price of a person among the people of Israel.
> They paid it for a potter's field,
>   as the Lord had commanded me." [199]

5.49 Jesus Before Pilate

It was early in the morning when Jesus was taken from Caiaphas to the building where the Roman governor stayed. But the crowd waited outside. Any of them who had gone inside would have become unclean and would not be allowed to eat the Passover meal.

Pilate came out and asked, "What charges are you bringing against this man?"

They answered, "He is a criminal! That's why we brought him to you."

Pilate told them, "Take him and judge him by your own laws."

The crowd replied, "We are not allowed to put anyone to death." And so what Jesus said about his death would soon come true.

Pilate then went back inside. He called Jesus over and asked, "Are you the king of the Jews?"

Jesus answered, "Are you asking this on your own or did someone tell you about me?"

"You know I'm not a Jew!" Pilate said. "Your own people and the chief priests brought you to me. What have you done?"

Jesus answered, "My kingdom doesn't belong to this world. If it did, my followers would have fought to keep me from being handed over to the Jewish leaders. No, my kingdom doesn't belong to this world."

"So you are a king," Pilate replied.

"You are saying that I am a king," Jesus told him. "I was born into this world to tell about the truth. And everyone who belongs to the truth knows my voice."

Pilate asked Jesus, "What is truth?"

Pilate went back out and said, "I don't find this man guilty of anything!" [200]

They started accusing him and said, "We caught this man trying to get our people to riot and to stop paying taxes to the Emperor. He also claims that he is the Messiah, our king." [201]

Then Pilate questioned him again, "Don't you have anything to say? Don't you hear what crimes they say you have done?" But Jesus did not answer, and Pilate was amazed.[202]

But they all kept on saying, "He has been teaching and causing trouble all over Judea. He started in Galilee and has now come all the way here."

When Pilate heard this, he asked, "Is this man from Galilee?" After Pilate learned that Jesus came from the region ruled by Herod, he sent him to Herod, who was in Jerusalem at that time.

5.50 Jesus Before Herod

For a long time Herod had wanted to see Jesus and was very happy because he finally had this chance. He had heard many things about Jesus and hoped to see him work a miracle.

Herod asked him a lot of questions, but Jesus did not answer. Then the chief priests and the teachers of the Law of Moses stood up and accused him of all kinds of bad things.

Herod and his soldiers made fun of Jesus and insulted him. They put a fine robe on him and sent him back to Pilate. That same day Herod and Pilate became friends, even though they had been enemies before this.[203]

5.51 Jesus Again Before Pilate

During Passover, Pilate always freed one prisoner chosen by the people. And at that time there was a prisoner named Barabbas. He and some others had been arrested for murder during a riot. The crowd now came and asked Pilate to set a prisoner free, just as he usually did.[204]

Pilate called together the chief priests, the leaders, and the people. He told them, "You brought Jesus to me and said he was a troublemaker. But I have questioned him here in front of you, and I have not found him guilty of anything that you say he has done. Herod didn't find him guilty either and sent him back. This man doesn't deserve to be put to death!"[205]

So when the crowd came together, Pilate asked them, "Which prisoner do you want me to set free? Do you want Jesus Barabbas or Jesus who is called the Messiah?" Pilate knew that the leaders had brought Jesus to him because they were jealous.

While Pilate was judging the case, his wife sent him a message. It said, "Don't have anything to do with that innocent man. I have had nightmares because of him."

But the chief priests and the leaders convinced the crowds to ask for

Barabbas to be set free and for Jesus to be killed. Pilate asked the crowd again, "Which of these two men do you want me to set free?"

"Barabbas!" they replied. [206]

Jesus Sentenced to be Crucified

Pilate gave orders for Jesus to be beaten with a whip. The soldiers made a crown out of thorn branches and put it on Jesus. Then they put a purple robe on him. They came up to him and said, "Hey, you king of the Jews!" They also hit him with their fists.

Once again Pilate went out. This time he said, "I will have Jesus brought out to you again. Then you can see for yourselves that I have not found him guilty."

Jesus came out, wearing the crown of thorns and the purple robe. Pilate said, "Here is the man!"

When the chief priests and the temple police saw him, they yelled, "Nail him to a cross! Nail him to a cross!"

Pilate told them, "You take him and nail him to a cross! I don't find him guilty of anything."

The crowd replied, "He claimed to be the Son of God! Our Jewish Law says that he must be put to death."

When Pilate heard this, he was terrified. He went back inside and asked Jesus, "Where are you from?" But Jesus did not answer.

"Why won't you answer my question?" Pilate asked. "Don't you know that I have the power to let you go free or to nail you to a cross?"

Jesus replied, "If God had not given you the power, you couldn't do anything at all to me. But the one who handed me over to you did something even worse."

Then Pilate wanted to set Jesus free. But the crowd again yelled, "If you set this man free, you are no friend of the Emperor! Anyone who claims to be a king is an enemy of the Emperor."

When Pilate heard this, he brought Jesus out. Then he sat down on the judge's bench at the place known as "The Stone Pavement." In Aramaic this pavement is called "Gabbatha." It was about noon on the day before Passover, and Pilate said to the crowd, "Look at your king!"

"Kill him! Kill him!" they yelled. "Nail him to a cross!"

"So you want me to nail your king to a cross?" Pilate asked.

The chief priests replied, "The Emperor is our king!" [207]

Pilate saw that there was nothing he could do and that the people were starting to riot. So he took some water and washed his hands in front of them and said, "I won't have anything to do with killing this man. You are the ones doing it!"

Everyone answered, "We and our own families will take the blame for his death!" [208]

Finally, Pilate gave in. He freed the man who was in jail for rioting and murder, because he was the one the crowd wanted to be set free. Then Pilate handed Jesus over for them to do what they wanted with him. [209]

5.53 The Soldiers Mock Jesus

The governor's soldiers led Jesus into the fortress and brought together the rest of the troops. They stripped off Jesus' clothes and put a scarlet robe on him. They made a crown out of thorn branches and placed it on his head, and they put a stick in his right hand. The soldiers knelt down and pretended to worship him. They made fun of him and shouted, "Hey, you king of the Jews!" Then they spit on him. They took the stick from him and beat him on the head with it.

When the soldiers had finished making fun of Jesus, they took off the robe. They put his own clothes back on him and led him off to be nailed to a cross. [210]

5.54 The Crucifixion

As Jesus was being led away, some soldiers grabbed hold of a man from Cyrene named Simon. He was coming in from the fields, but they put the cross on him and made him carry it behind Jesus.

A large crowd was following Jesus, and in the crowd a lot of women were crying and weeping for him. Jesus turned to the women and said:

> Women of Jerusalem, don't cry for me! Cry for yourselves and for your children. Someday people will say, "Women who never had children are really fortunate!" At that time everyone will say to the mountains, "Fall on us!" They will say to the hills, "Hide us!" If this can happen when the wood is green, what do you think will happen when it is dry?

Two criminals were led out to be put to death with Jesus. [211]

They came to a place named Golgotha, which means "Place of a Skull." There they gave Jesus some wine mixed with a drug to ease the pain. But when Jesus tasted what it was, he refused to drink it. [212]

When the soldiers came to the place called "The Skull," they nailed Jesus to a cross. They also nailed the two criminals to crosses, one on each side of Jesus.

Jesus said, "Father, forgive these people! They don't know what they're doing." [213]

After the soldiers had nailed Jesus to the cross, they divided up his clothes into four parts, one for each of them. But his outer garment was made from a single piece of cloth, and it did not have any seams. The soldiers said to each other, "Let's not rip it apart. We will gamble to see who gets it." This happened so that the Scriptures would come true, which say,

> "They divided up my clothes
>   and gambled for my garments."

The soldiers then did what they had decided. [214]

Pilate ordered the charge against Jesus to be written on a board and put above the cross. It read, "Jesus of Nazareth, King of the Jews." The words were written in Hebrew, Latin, and Greek.

The place where Jesus was taken wasn't far from the city, and many of the Jewish people read the charge against him. So the chief priests went to Pilate and said, "Why did you write that he is King of the Jews? You should have written, 'He claimed to be King of the Jews.'"

But Pilate told them, "What is written will not be changed!" [215]

People who passed by said terrible things about Jesus. They shook their heads and shouted, "So you're the one who claimed you could tear down the temple and build it again in three days! If you are God's Son, save yourself and come down from the cross!"

The chief priests, the leaders, and the teachers of the Law of Moses also made fun of Jesus. They said, "He saved others, but he can't save himself. If he is the king of Israel, he should come down from the cross! Then we will believe him. He trusted God, so let God save him, if he wants to. He even said he was God's Son." [216]

One of the criminals hanging there also insulted Jesus by saying, "Aren't you the Messiah? Save yourself and save us!"

But the other criminal told the first one off, "Don't you fear God? Aren't you getting the same punishment as this man? We got what was coming to us, but he didn't do anything wrong." Then he said to Jesus, "Remember me when you come into power!"

Jesus replied, "I promise that today you will be with me in paradise." [217]

Jesus' mother stood beside his cross with her sister and Mary the wife of Clopas. Mary Magdalene was standing there too. When Jesus saw his mother and his favorite disciple with her, he said to his mother, "This man is now your son." Then he said to the disciple, "She is now your mother." From then on, that disciple took her into his own home. [218]

5.55 The Death of Jesus

At noon the sky turned dark and stayed that way until three o'clock. Then about that time Jesus shouted, "Eli, Eli, lema sabachthani?" which means, "My God, my God, why have you deserted me?"

Some of the people standing there heard Jesus and said, "He's calling for Elijah." [219]

Jesus knew that he had now finished his work. And in order to make the Scriptures come true, he said, "I am thirsty!" A jar of cheap wine was there. Someone then soaked a sponge with the wine and held it up to Jesus' mouth on the stem of a hyssop plant. After Jesus drank the wine, he said, "Everything is done!" [220]

Jesus shouted, "Father, I put myself in your hands!" Then he died. [221]

At once the curtain in the temple was torn in two from top to bottom. The earth shook, and rocks split apart. Graves opened, and many of God's people were raised to life. Then after Jesus had risen to life, they came out of their graves and they went to the holy city, where they were seen by many people.

The officer and the soldiers guarding Jesus felt the earthquake and saw everything else that happened. They were frightened and said, "This man really was God's Son!"[222]

The next day would be both a Sabbath and the Passover. It was a special day for the Jewish people, and they did not want the bodies to stay on the crosses during that day. So they asked Pilate to break the men's legs and take their bodies down. The soldiers first broke the legs of the other two men who were nailed there. But when they came to Jesus, they saw that he was already dead, and they did not break his legs.

One of the soldiers stuck his spear into Jesus' side, and blood and water came out. We know this is true, because it was told by someone who saw it happen. Now you can have faith too. All this happened so that the Scriptures would come true, which say, "No bone of his body will be broken" and, "They will see the one in whose side they stuck a spear."

5.56 The Burial of Jesus

Joseph from Arimathea was one of Jesus' disciples. He had kept it secret though, because he was afraid of the Jewish leaders. But now he asked Pilate to let him have Jesus' body. Pilate gave him permission, and Joseph took it down from the cross.

Nicodemus also came with about seventy-five pounds of spices made from myrrh and aloes. This was the same Nicodemus who had visited Jesus one night. The two men wrapped the body in a linen cloth, together with the spices, which was how the Jewish people buried their dead.²²³

Then Joseph put the body in his own tomb that had been cut into solid rock and had never been used. He rolled a big stone against the entrance to the tomb and went away.²²⁴

Mary Magdalene and Mary the mother of Joseph were watching and saw where the body was placed.²²⁵

Then they went to prepare some sweet-smelling spices for his burial. But on the Sabbath they rested, as the Law of Moses commands.²²⁶

5.57 The Guard at the Tomb

On the next day, which was a Sabbath, the chief priests and the Pharisees went together to Pilate. They said, "Sir, we remember what that liar said while he was still alive. He claimed that in three days he would come back from death. So please order the tomb to be carefully guarded for three days. If you don't, his disciples may come and steal his body. They will tell the people that he has been raised to life, and this last lie will be worse than the first one."

Pilate said to them, "All right, take some of your soldiers and guard the tomb as well as you know how." So they sealed it tight and placed soldiers there to guard it.²²⁷

You always work as a group, not somebody just singled out. There is no such thing as that with the Apache. We say "I walk with you" not "I walk before you" or "I walk behind you" ... You are a leader, you are apart.
Philip Cassadore, Apache

REVIEW QUESTIONS, SECTION 5

1. Many believed in Jesus but they would not tell anyone for they liked praise from _____ more than praise from _____. (5.5)

2. Jesus said that if you want the Father to forgive your sins, when you stand to pray you must _____ what others have done to you. (5.6)

3. In response to the Pharisees and the followers of Herod Jesus said, Give to the Emperor what belongs to him and _____ God what belongs to God. (5.11)

4. Jesus called attention to the offering of the poor widow because she is very poor and gave _____ she had. (5.16)

5. Jesus warned that false prophets will come and fool people. Evil will spread and cause many people to stop _____ others. If we will be ____-_____ to the _____ we will be saved. (5.17)

6. Always be _____! You don't know when the Son of Man will come. (5.18)

7. Those who have failed to help God's people will be _____ forever, but the ones who have _____ God will have eternal _____. (5.21)

8. As their Lord and _____, Jesus said to His disciples that He had washed their feet to set them an _____ that they should do the same for each other. (5.26)

9. When Thomas asked how the disciples could know the way, Jesus answered, "I am the way, the _____ and the life. Without me no one can go to the _____." (5.32)

10. Is it possible to spend a long time with Jesus without really knowing him? Yes ___ No ___ (5.32)

11. While comparing Himself to the vine and His disciples to the _____, Jesus told them that apart from Him they could do nothing, but if they stayed joined to Him they would produce lots of _____. (5.34)

12. Jesus commanded His disciples, whom He called friends, to love each other as He had loved them, and told them the greatest way to show love is to die for _____. (5.34)

13. The Spirit shows what is truth and will _____ you into full truth. (5.36)

14. In His prayer to the Father, Jesus said, "Eternal life is to _____ the only true God, and Jesus Christ. " (5.38)

15. Could Jesus have asked His Father to deliver him from his enemies, suffering, and death? Yes____ No ____ (5.42)

16. What did Jesus tell the thief who recognized his own sin and Jesus' innocence, and asked Jesus to remember him? " I promise that today you will be with Me in _____." (5.54)

17. What did the Roman officer and those with him who were guarding Jesus say? "This man really was _____ Son." (5.55)

> This covers it all, the Earth and the Most High Power whose ways are beautiful
> All is beautiful before me,
> All is beautiful behind me,
> All is beautiful above me,
> All is beautiful around me.
> **Navajo Song**

6 The Last Forty Days

6.1 The Resurrection

After the Sabbath, [228] suddenly a strong earthquake struck, and the Lord's angel came down from heaven. He rolled away the stone and sat on it. The angel looked as bright as lightning, and his clothes were white as snow. The guards shook from fear and fell down, as though they were dead. [229]

Mary Magdalene, Salome, and Mary the mother of James bought some spices to put on Jesus' body. Very early on Sunday morning, just as the sun was coming up, they went to the tomb. On their way, they were asking one another, "Who will roll the stone away from the entrance for us?" But when they looked, they saw that the stone had already been rolled away. And it was a huge stone![230]

They went in. But they did not find the body of the Lord Jesus, and they did not know what to think.

Suddenly two men in shining white clothes stood beside them. The women were afraid and bowed to the ground. [231]

The man said, "Don't be alarmed! You are looking for Jesus from Nazareth, who was nailed to a cross."[232]

But the men said, "Why are you looking in the place of the dead for someone who is alive?[233] God has raised him to life, and he isn't here. You can see the place where they put his body.[234] Jesus isn't here! He has been raised from death. Remember that while he was still in Galilee, he told you, 'The Son of Man will be handed over to sinners who will nail him to a cross. But three days later he will rise to life.' [235]

Now go and tell his disciples, and especially Peter, that he will go ahead of you to Galilee. You will see him there, just as he told you."[236]

Then they remembered what Jesus had said.[237]

The women were frightened and yet very happy, as they hurried from the tomb and ran to tell his disciples.[238]

Mary Magdalene, Joanna, Mary the mother of James, and some other women were the ones who had gone to the tomb. When they returned, they told the eleven apostles and the others what had happened. The apostles thought it was all nonsense, and they would not believe.

But [239] Peter and the other disciple started for the tomb. They ran side by side, until the other disciple ran faster than Peter and got there first. He bent over and saw the strips of linen cloth lying inside the tomb, but he did not go in.

When Simon Peter got there, he went into the tomb and saw the strips of cloth. He also saw the piece of cloth that had been used to cover Jesus' face. It was rolled up and in a place by itself. The disciple who got there first then went into the tomb, and when he saw it, he believed. At that time Peter and the other disciple did not know that the Scriptures said Jesus would rise to life. So the two of them went back to the other disciples. [240]

6.2 Jesus Appears to Mary Magdalene

Very early on the first day of the week, after Jesus had risen to life, he appeared to Mary Magdalene. Earlier he had forced seven demons out of her.[241]

Mary Magdalene stood crying outside the tomb. She was still weeping, when she stooped down and saw two angels inside. They were dressed in white and were sitting where Jesus' body had been. One was at the head and the other was at the foot. The angels asked Mary, "Why are you crying?"

She answered, "They have taken away my Lord's body! I don't know where they have put him."

As soon as Mary said this, she turned around and saw Jesus standing there. But she did not know who he was. Jesus asked her, "Why are you crying? Who are you looking for?"

She thought he was the gardener and said, "Sir, if you have taken his body away, please tell me, so I can go and get him."

Then Jesus said to her, "Mary!"

She turned and said to him, "Rabboni." The Aramaic word "Rabboni" means "Teacher."

Jesus told her, "Don't hold on to me! I have not yet gone to the Father. But tell my disciples that I am going to the one who is my Father and my God, as well as your Father and your God." Mary Magdalene then went and told the disciples that she had seen the Lord. She also told them what he had said to her.[242]

Even though they heard that Jesus was alive and that Mary had seen him, they would not believe it.[243]

6.3 Jesus Appears to Others

Suddenly Jesus met them and greeted them. They went near him, held on to his feet, and worshiped him. Then Jesus said, "Don't be afraid! Tell my followers to go to Galilee. They will see me there."

6.4 The Guard's Report

While the women were on their way, some soldiers who had been guarding the tomb went into the city. They told the chief priests everything that had happened. So the chief priests met with the leaders and decided to bribe the soldiers with a lot of money. They said to the soldiers, "Tell everyone that Jesus' disciples came during the night and stole his body while you were asleep. If the governor hears about this, we will talk to him. You won't have anything to worry about." The soldiers took the money and did what they were told. The Jewish people still tell each other this story.[244]

6.5 On the Road to Emmaus

That same day two of Jesus' disciples were going to the village of Emmaus, which was about seven miles from Jerusalem. As they were talking and thinking about what had happened, Jesus came near and started walking along beside them. But they did not know who he was.

Jesus asked them, "What were you talking about as you walked along?"

The two of them stood there looking sad and gloomy. Then the one named Cleopas asked Jesus, "Are you the only person from Jerusalem who didn't know what was happening there these last few days?"

"What do you mean?" Jesus asked.

They answered:

> Those things that happened to Jesus from Nazareth. By what he did and said he showed that he was a powerful prophet, who pleased God and all the people. Then the chief priests and our leaders had him arrested and sentenced to die on a cross. We had hoped that he would be the one to set Israel free! But it has already been three days since all this happened.
>
> Some women in our group surprised us. They had gone to the tomb early in the morning, but did not find the body of Jesus. They came back, saying that they had seen a vision of angels who told them that he is alive. Some men from our group went to the tomb and found it just as the women had said. But they didn't see Jesus either.

Then Jesus asked the two disciples, "Why can't you understand? How can you be so slow to believe all that the prophets said? Didn't you know that the Messiah would have to suffer before he was given his glory?" Jesus then explained everything written about himself in the Scriptures, beginning with the Law of Moses and the Books of the Prophets.

When the two of them came near the village where they were going, Jesus seemed to be going farther. They begged him, "Stay with us! It's already late, and the sun is going down." So Jesus went into the house to stay with them.

After Jesus sat down to eat, he took some bread. He blessed it and broke it. Then he gave it to them. At once they knew who he was, but he disappeared. They said to each other, "When he talked with us along the road and explained the Scriptures to us, didn't it warm our hearts?" So they got right up and returned to Jerusalem.

The two disciples found the eleven apostles and the others gathered together. And they learned from the group that the Lord was really alive and had appeared to Peter. Then the disciples from Emmaus told what happened on the road and how they knew he was the Lord when he broke the bread.[245]

6.6 Jesus Appears to His Disciples

The disciples were afraid of the Jewish leaders, and on the evening of that same Sunday they locked themselves in a room.[246]

While Jesus' disciples were talking about what had happened, Jesus appeared and greeted them. They were frightened and terrified because they thought they were seeing a ghost.[247]

He scolded them because they were too stubborn to believe the ones who had seen him after he had been raised to life.[248]

But Jesus said, "Why are you so frightened? Why do you doubt? Look at my hands and my feet and see who I am! Touch me and find out for yourselves. Ghosts don't have flesh and bones as you see I have."

After Jesus said this, he showed them his hands and his feet. The disciples were so glad and amazed that they could not believe it. Jesus then asked them, "Do you have something to eat?" They gave him a piece of baked fish. He took it and ate it as they watched.[249]

When the disciples saw the Lord, they became very happy.

After Jesus had greeted them again, he said, "I am sending you, just as the Father has sent me." Then he breathed on them and said, "Receive the Holy Spirit. If you forgive anyone's sins, they will be forgiven. But if you don't forgive their sins, they will not be forgiven."

6.7 Jesus Appears to Thomas

Although Thomas the Twin was one of the twelve disciples, he wasn't with the others when Jesus appeared to them. So they told him, "We have seen the Lord!"

But Thomas said, "First, I must see the nail scars in his hands and touch them with my finger. I must put my hand where the spear went into his side. I won't believe unless I do this!"

A week later the disciples were together again. This time, Thomas was with them. Jesus came in while the doors were still locked and stood in the middle of the group. He greeted his disciples and said to Thomas, "Put your finger here and look at my hands! Put your hand into my side. Stop doubting and have faith!"

Thomas replied, "You are my Lord and my God!"

Jesus said, "Thomas, do you have faith because you have seen me? The people who have faith in me without seeing me are the ones who are really blessed!"[250]

6.8 Jesus and the Miraculous Catch of Fish

Jesus later appeared to his disciples along the shore of Lake Tiberias. Simon Peter, Thomas the Twin, Nathanael from Cana in Galilee, and the brothers James and John, were there, together with two other disciples. Simon Peter said, "I'm going fishing!"

The others said, "We will go with you." They went out in their boat. But they didn't catch a thing that night.

Early the next morning Jesus stood on the shore, but the disciples did not realize who he was. Jesus shouted, "Friends, have you caught anything?"

"No!" they answered.

So he told them, "Let your net down on the right side of your boat, and you will catch some fish."

They did, and the net was so full of fish that they could not drag it up into the boat.

Jesus' favorite disciple told Peter, "It's the Lord!" When Simon heard that it was the Lord, he put on the clothes that he had taken off while he was working. Then he jumped into the water. The boat was only about a hundred yards from shore. So the other disciples stayed in the boat and dragged in the net full of fish.

When the disciples got out of the boat, they saw some bread and a charcoal fire with fish on it. Jesus told his disciples, "Bring some of the fish you just caught." Simon Peter got back into the boat and dragged the net to shore. In it were one hundred fifty-three large fish, but still the net did not rip.

Jesus said, "Come and eat!" But none of the disciples dared ask who he was. They knew he was the Lord. Jesus took the bread in his hands and gave some of it to his disciples. He did the same with the fish. This was the third time that Jesus appeared to his disciples after he was raised from death.

6.9 Jesus Reinstates Peter

When Jesus and his disciples had finished eating, he asked, "Simon son of John, do you love me more than the others do?"

Simon Peter answered, "Yes, Lord, you know I do!"

"Then feed my lambs," Jesus said.

Jesus asked a second time, "Simon son of John, do you love me?"

Peter answered, "Yes, Lord, you know I love you!"

"Then take care of my sheep," Jesus told him.

Jesus asked a third time, "Simon son of John, do you love me?"

Peter was hurt because Jesus had asked him three times if he loved him. So he told Jesus, "Lord, you know everything. You know I love you."

Jesus replied, "Feed my sheep. I tell you for certain that when you were a young man, you dressed yourself and went wherever you wanted to go. But when you are old, you will hold out your hands. Then others will wrap your belt around you and lead you where you don't want to go."

Jesus said this to tell how Peter would die and bring honor to God. Then he said to Peter, "Follow me!"

Peter turned and saw Jesus' favorite disciple following them. He was the same one who had sat next to Jesus at the meal and had asked, "Lord, who is going to betray you?" When Peter saw that disciple, he asked Jesus, "Lord, what about him?"

Jesus answered, "What is it to you, if I want him to live until I return? You must follow me." So the rumor spread among the other disciples that this disciple would not die. But Jesus did not say he would not die. He simply said, "What is it to you, if I want him to live until I return?"[251]

6.10 The Great Commission

Jesus' eleven disciples went to a mountain in Galilee, where Jesus had told them to meet him. They saw him and worshiped him, but some of them doubted.

Jesus came to them and said:

I have been given all authority in heaven and on earth! Go to the people of all nations and make them my disciples. Baptize them in the name of the Father, the Son, and the Holy Spirit, and teach them to do everything I have told you.[252]

Anyone who believes me and is baptized will be saved. But anyone who refuses to believe me will be condemned. Everyone who believes me will be able to do wonderful things. By using my name they will force out demons, and they will speak new languages. They will handle snakes and will drink poison and not be hurt. They will also heal sick people by placing their hands on them.[253]

I will be with you always, even until the end of the world.[254]

6.11 Final Instructions

For forty days after Jesus had suffered and died, he proved in many ways that he had been raised from death. He appeared to his apostles and spoke to them about God's kingdom. While he was still with them,[255] Jesus said to them, "While I was still with you, I told you that everything written about me in the Law of Moses, the Books of the Prophets, and in the Psalms had to happen."

Then he helped them understand the Scriptures. He told them:

> The Scriptures say that the Messiah must suffer, then three days later he will rise from death. They also say that all people of every nation must be told in my name to turn to God, in order to be forgiven. So beginning in Jerusalem, you must tell everything that has happened. I will send you the one my Father has promised, but you must stay in the city until you are given power from heaven.[256]
>
> Don't leave Jerusalem yet. Wait here for the Father to give you the Holy Spirit, just as I told you he has promised to do. John baptized with water, but in a few days you will be baptized with the Holy Spirit.

While the apostles were still with Jesus, they asked him, "Lord, are you now going to give Israel its own king again?"

Jesus said to them, "You don't need to know the time of those events that only the Father controls. But the Holy Spirit will come upon you and give you power. Then you will tell everyone about me in Jerusalem, in all Judea, in Samaria, and everywhere in the world."[257]

6.12 The Ascension to Heaven

Jesus led his disciples out to Bethany, where he raised his hands and blessed them. As he was doing this, he left and was taken up to heaven.[258]

They could not see him, but as he went up, they kept looking up into the sky.

Suddenly two men dressed in white clothes were standing there beside them. They said, "Why are you men from Galilee standing here and looking up into the sky? Jesus has been taken to heaven. But he will come back in the same way that you have seen him go."[259]

After the Lord Jesus had said these things to the disciples, he was taken back up to heaven where he sat down at the right side of God.[260]

After his disciples had worshiped him, they returned to Jerusalem and were very happy.[261] The Mount of Olives was about half a mile from Jerusalem.[262]

They spent their time in the temple, praising God.[263]

6.13 The Holy Spirit Comes at Pentecost

On the day of Pentecost all the Lord's followers were together in one place. Suddenly there was a noise from heaven like the sound of a mighty wind! It filled the house where they were meeting. Then they saw what looked like fiery tongues moving in all directions, and a tongue came and settled on each person there. The Holy Spirit took control of everyone, and they began speaking whatever languages the Spirit let them speak.

Many religious Jews from every country in the world were living in Jerusalem. And when they heard this noise, a crowd gathered. But they were surprised, because they were hearing everything in their own languages. They were excited and amazed, and said:

> Don't all these who are speaking come from Galilee? Then why do we hear them speaking our very own languages? Some of us are from Parthia, Media, and Elam. Others are from Mesopotamia, Judea, Cappadocia, Pontus, Asia, Phrygia, Pamphylia, Egypt, parts of Libya near Cyrene, Rome, Crete, and Arabia. Some of us were born Jews, and others of us have chosen to be Jews. Yet we all hear them using our own languages to tell the wonderful things God has done.[264]

6.14 Conclusion

Then the disciples left and preached everywhere. The Lord was with them, and the miracles they worked proved that their message was true.[265]

Jesus did many other things. If they were all written in books, I don't suppose there would be room enough in the whole world for all the books.[266]

Jesus worked many other miracles for his disciples, and not all of them are written in this book. But these are written so that you will put your faith in Jesus as the Messiah and the Son of God. If you have faith in him, you will have true life.[267]

We did not think of the great open plains, the beautiful rolling hills and the winding streams and tangled growth as "wild." To us it was tame. Earth was bountiful and we were surrounded with the blessings of the Great Mystery.

**Luther Standing Bear
Rosebud Sioux**

REVIEW QUESTIONS, SECTION 6

1. After His resurrection, Jesus said to Thomas, "Do you have _____ because you have seen Me? The people who have faith in Me without seeing Me are the ones who really _____." (6.7)

2. Before being taken up into heaven, Jesus told His disciples He would be with them always to the end of the _____. (6.10)

3. Jesus told His followers to wait in Jerusalem so they could be _____ with the Holy Spirit. Then they would tell _____ about Jesus. (6.11)

4. Was everything Jesus did written down? Yes ____ No _____ The purpose of the miraculous signs Jesus did that were written in this Book is so that the reader may have faith that Jesus is the _____ and the _____ of God, and that by faith in Jesus you have _____ life. (6.14)

> What is life?
> It is the flash of a firefly in
>   the night.
> It is the breath of a buffalo in
>   the wintertime.
> It is the little shadow which
>   runs across
> the grass and loses itself in
>   the sunset.
> **Crowfoot, Blackfoot warrior and orator 1830 – 1890**

The Ancestors of Jesus, According to Matthew

Jesus Christ came from the family of King David and also from the family of Abraham. And this is a list of his ancestors. From Abraham to King David, his ancestors were:

Abraham, Isaac, Jacob, Judah and his brothers (Judah's sons were Perez and Zerah, and their mother was Tamar), Hezron;

Ram, Amminadab, Nahshon, Salmon, Boaz (his mother was Rahab), Obed (his mother was Ruth), Jesse, and King David.

From David to the time of the exile in Babylonia, the ancestors of Jesus were:

David, Solomon (his mother had been Uriah's wife), Rehoboam, Abijah, Asa, Jehoshaphat, Jehoram;

Uzziah, Jotham, Ahaz, Hezekiah, Manasseh, Amon, Josiah, and Jehoiachin and his brothers.

From the exile to the birth of Jesus, his ancestors were:

Jehoiachin, Shealtiel, Zerubbabel, Abiud, Eliakim, Azor, Zadok, Achim;

Eliud, Eleazar, Matthan, Jacob, and Joseph, the husband of Mary, the mother of Jesus, who is called the Messiah.

There were fourteen generations from Abraham to David. There were also fourteen from David to the exile in Babylonia and fourteen more to the birth of the Messiah.

The Ancestors of Jesus, According to Luke

When Jesus began to preach, he was about thirty years old. Everyone thought he was the son of Joseph. But his family went back through Heli, Matthat, Levi, Melchi, Jannai, Joseph Mattathias, Amos, Nahum, Esli, Nagga Maath, Mattathias, Semein, Josech, Joda;

Joanan, Rhesa, Zerubbabel, Shealtiel, Neri Melchi, Addi, Cosam, Elmadam, Er, Joshua, Eliezer, Jorim, Matthat, Levi;

Simeon, Judah, Joseph, Jonam, Eliakim Melea, Menna, Mattatha, Nathan, David, Jesse, Obed, Boaz, Salmon, Nahshon;

Amminadab, Admin, Arni, Hezron, Perez, Judah, Jacob, Isaac, Abraham, Terah, Nahor, Serug, Reu, Peleg, Eber, Shelah;

Cainan, Arphaxad, Shem, Noah, Lamech, Methuselah, Enoch, Jared, Mahalaleel, Kenan, Enosh, and Seth.

The family of Jesus went all the way back to Adam and then to God.

May the Warm Winds of Heaven
Blow softly upon your house.
May the Great Spirit
Bless all who enter there.
May your Mocassins
Make happy tracks
in many snows,
and may the Rainbow
Always touch your shoulder.
Cherokee Prayer Blessing

Timeline of the Life of Christ

The following chart contains information which has been uncovered by Bible scholars from all around the world. Although not everyone agrees on these exact dates, most of the evidence found so far does lead to these conclusions. This information is very useful because it gives a better idea about when Jesus actually lived, ministered, and died.

Date	Event
6 or 5 B.C.	Birth of Christ
4 B.C.	Death of Herod the Great
12 AD	Beginning of the reign of Tiberius Caesar
26 AD.	Beginning of the ministry of John the Baptist early in the year
	Baptism of Christ
	Beginning of the ministry of Christ late in the year
27 AD.	First Passover during the ministry of Christ
28 AD.	Second Passover during the ministry of Christ
29 AD.	Third Passover during the ministry of Christ
30 AD.	Crucifixion of Christ (Nisan/April 14)

We have lived on this land from the days beyond history's record, far past any living memory, deep into the time of legend. The story of my people and the story of this place are one single story. We are always joined together.
Pueblo Elder

DICTIONARY

altar – a raised platform, made of stones, metal, dirt or wood, on which sacrifices were made.

angel – a heavenly being.

apostle – 1. the twelve men Jesus chose to work with him during his earthly ministry; after being equipped by the Holy Spirit, they were sent out to preach about Jesus.
2. later, someone who had been with Jesus, had seen his miracles and then taught others about him.

Aramaic – the main language used in the countries east of the Mediterranean Sea during Jesus' earthly ministry.

baptize – a religious ceremony in which water is used as a symbol of cleansing from sin. Baptism is a sign that our sins are washed away and that Jesus has taken us to be his own.

betray – to turn a friend over to his or her enemies; to be unfaithful to.

bless – 1. to make holy; 2. to show favor to; 3. to ask God to show favor to.

burden – a heavy load.

Caesar – the title of many Roman emperors.

Christ – the official title of Jesus. meaning "the Anointed One." It is a Greek word, and it means the same as the Hebrew word Messiah.

circumcise – to cut off the loose fold of skin at the end of the penis.

commandment – an order given by God. God gave the Ten Commandments to the Israelites while they were encamped in the area of Mount Sinai.

condemn – to give out punishment to; to pronounce guilty.

curse – (v.) to ask God to bring evil or injury to; (n.) a prayer or desire that evil or injury come upon someone.

debt – something that one person owes another.

deceive – (v.) to fool or trick; to lie (n. deceit, deception; adj. deceitful).

demon – evil spirit. A demon-possessed person is one who is controlled by evil spirits.

disciple – a follower or student, especially one who believes what the leader teaches. Anyone who believes in Jesus is his disciple.

envy – to want for yourself something that belongs to another person.

eternal – without beginning or end; forever; timeless. God is eternal.

everlasting – forever; without end.

evil – wicked; doing things against God's will.

faith – belief and trust in God; knowing that God is real, even though we can't see him.

faithful – trustworthy, loyal. God is faithful.

fig – 1. a brownish pear-shaped fruit that grows in countries near the Mediterranean Sea; 2. the tree that grows this fruit.

forgive – to pardon or excuse; no longer to blame or be angry with someone who had done you wrong.

fruitful – productive; yielding much fruit.

genealogy – a list of a person's ancestors or descendants; a family tree.

generation – the entire number of people born and living at about the same time. Grandparents, parents and children are three different generations.

glory – 1. honor; praise; 2. a source of pride or worthiness.

Golgotha – the hill outside Jerusalem where Jesus was hung on a cross.

gospel – 1. the good news that Jesus died for our sins and rose again; 2. Gospel, any of the first four books of the New Testament.

guilty – having broken a law or commandment; deserving punishment.

Herod – the family name of five kings who ruled Palestine under the Roman emperor.

high priest – the chief religious official in the Jewish religion. In the Old Testament he offered the most important sacrifices to God on behalf of the people. In Jesus' time he was also the head of the Sanhedrin (the highest Jewish court), and a powerful political leader – even having a small army.

holy – (v.) set apart for God; (adj.) belonging to God; pure; godly

Holy Spirit – the third person of the Trinity; the Spirit lives and works in our hearts and minds. Jesus promised his disciples that he would send his Spirit (Jn 14:16-26), and it came at Pentecost in a powerful way (Ac 2). Other names are: the Spirit, Counselor and Comforter.

humble – (v.) to make humble in spirit or manner; (adj.) not proud; not pretending to be important.

hymn – a song of praise to God.

hyssop – a plant used to sprinkle water or blood for religious cleansing.

incense – 1. spices burned to make a sweet-smelling smoke, as a way of worshipping God; 2. the sweet smell of the smoke of burning spices.

Jew – an Israelite; one of the chosen people of God; a descendant of Abraham through Jacob.

judge – to decide if something is good or bad; to condemn.

kingdom of heaven – (also called, kingdom of God) – God's rule in the lives of his chosen people in his creation. Anyone who is born again by believing in Jesus enters this kingdom.

Lamb of God – a name for Jesus that reminds us that he is like the lambs offered for sacrifice in the Old Testament.

law – 1. God's rules, which help his people know what is right and wrong. The Ten Commandments are part of God's law; 2. Law, the five first books of the Bible, written by Moses.

leprosy – a word used in the Bible for many different skin diseases and infections.

locusts – a type of grasshopper. When they would settle in a grain field, orchard or other cultivated area in Bible times, they could devastate the crop.

manna – the special food God gave daily to the Israelites until they reached the promised land.

mercy – kindness and forgiveness, especially when given to a person who doesn't deserve it.

Messiah – the "Anointed One"; Christ; the one the Jews expected to come and be their king.

miracle – an unusual happening, one that goes against the normal laws of nature. Miracles are done by the power of God.

myrrh – the sweet-smelling sap of myrrh bush. It was used to make the sacred anointing oil.

offering – 1. something given to God as an act of worship; 2. the killing of an animal to make the relationship between God and man right again. In the Old Testament, animals and grains were regularly used as offerings, in an attempt to bring the people closer to God.

paradise – a perfect place; heaven.

Passover – an annual Jewish holiday that yet today reminds the Jewish people of how God freed them from slavery in Egypt. At the Passover feast, the Jews eat bread made without yeast (unleavened bread), bitter herbs and lamb. With the unleavened bread they remember that they left Egypt hastily. There was no time to wait for yeast bread to rise. Bitter herbs remind them of their suffering in Egypt. The lamb reminds them of the lamb they killed at the first Passover and how they put its blood on the door frames. The Lord "passed over" the homes so marked, but he killed all the other firstborn in Egypt.

Pentecost – a Jewish feast celebrated fifty days after the Passover. Today the Christian church celebrates Pentecost because it was the day the Holy Spirit came to dwell with Christ's followers.

Pharisees – a group of Jews who obeyed very strictly both God's laws and all their own rules about God's laws.

priest – a Levite who offered sacrifices and prayers to God for the people.

prophet – a person who receives messages from God to tell to his people. A prophet is called by God to speak for him.

Sabbath – the seventh day of the week; the Jewish day of rest and worship. It extended from Friday sunset until Saturday sunset.

sackcloth – a rough cloth, usually woven from goats' hair. Clothing made of sackcloth was worn as a sign of mourning for the dead or as a sign that a person was sorry for his or her sins.

sacred – holy; set apart for God in a special way.

sacrifice – (v.) to offer as a sacrifice, (n.) an offering given to God for the sins of the people. In the Old Testament, God commanded the people to pay for their sins by sacrificing cattle, lambs, goats, doves or pigeons. The animals were killed, their blood splattered against the altar and their bodies burned on the altar. People who were very poor could bring flour to be burned on the altar. These sacrifices were pictures of Jesus' coming as a once-for-all sacrifice for sinners.

Sadducees – a group of Jewish leaders, many of them priests, who accepted only the written law of God. They opposed the Pharisees, who had many additional laws that had been passed down to them by their religious teachers. Unlike the Pharisees, the Sadducees did not believe in a resurrection of the dead, but they agreed with the Pharisees in their hatred of Jesus.

salvation – deliverance from the guilt and power of sin. By his death and resurrection, Jesus brings salvation to people who believe in him.

Samaritan – a person of late Old Testament or New Testament times who lived in or came from Samaria. The Samaritans were only partly Jewish, and they worshiped God differently than Jews in Israel. Jews from Judea and Galilee hated the Samaritans. They would go out of their way to travel around Samaria.

Sanhedrin – the ruling council of the Jews in Jesus' time. It was made up of seventy men, and the leader was the high priest. Even though the Romans had conquered Palestine and a Roman governor ruled the country, the Jews were allowed to judge many of their own matters. The Sanhedrin could decide whether someone was innocent or guilty of breaking a Jewish law, but it could not put anyone to death without the permission of the Roman governor.

Satan – the devil; the leader of the fallen spirits; the most powerful enemy of God and humans.

Savior – a name for Jesus that means he saves his people from sin.

scorpion – a spider-like animal with a poisonous stinger at the end of its tail.

Scripture – all or part of the Bible. When the Bible uses this word it means the Old Testament, since the New Testament had not yet been written. Today we call the Old and New Testaments the Bible or Scripture.

sin – (v.) to break the law of God; (n.) the act of not doing what God wants.

Sodom and Gomorrah – the two cities destroyed by God because the people were so wicked.

Son of Man – a name for Jesus. Jesus used this name to show he was the Messiah prophesied about in Daniel 7:13.

soul – the spiritual part of a person; the part of a person that does not die.

spirit – 1. the part of a person that is not the body; the soul; 2. beings who do not have bodies; 3. another name for the Holy Spirit.

stone – to kill or try to kill someone by throwing rocks or stones at him or her.

temple – 1. the place where the Jewish people worshiped and sacrificed in Jerusalem. The first temple was built by King Solomon as a house for God. 2. the human body.

tomb – a burial place. In Bible times, tombs often were either caves or were dug into stone cliffs.

virgin – a woman or girl who has never had sexual intercourse.

worship – (v.) to give praise, honor and respect to God; (n.) reverence to God.

yoke – 1. (v.) to join together; 2.(n.) a wooden bar that goes over the necks of two animals, usually oxen. The yoke holds the animals together as they pull an object, such as a plow or a cart.

When you are in doubt, be still, and wait;
when doubt no longer exists for you, then go
forward with courage.
So long as mists envelop you, be still;
be still until the sunlight pours through and
dispels the mists
-- as it surely will.
Then act with courage.

Humankind has not woven the web of life.
We are but one thread within it.
Whatever we do to the web, we do to ourselves.
All things are bound together.
All things connect.

Chief Seattle, 1854

INDEX

This Index will help you compare The Book of Hope with the Holy Bible. The sections of the Bible which have been put together in order are listed under each section of The Book of Hope, along with the footnote numbers which help to locate the verses in the Holy Bible. The numbered section headings appear in the same order as they are in the book. In this way the Index is also a complete outline of the book. The Numbers to the left of the Bible passage follow the same order in which they appear as footnotes in the Book of Hope.

SECTION 1.
The Thirty Years of Preparation

1.1 Introduction
    1 Mark 1:1
    2 Luke 1:1-4
    3 John 1:1-18
1.2 The Birth of John the Baptist Foretold
1.3 The Birth of Jesus Foretold
1.4 Mary Visits Elizabeth
1.5 Mary's Song
1.6 The Birth of John the Baptist
1.7 Zechariah Praises the Lord
    4 Luke 1:5-80
1.8 The Birth of Jesus
    5 Matthew 1:18-25a
1.9 The Shepherds and the Angels
1.10 Jesus Presented in the Temple
    6 Luke 2:1-38
1.11 The Visit of the Wise Men
1.12 The Escape to Egypt
1.13 The Killing of the Children
1.14 The Return to Nazareth
    7 Matthew 2:1-23
1.15 The Boy Jesus at the Temple

SECTION 2.
The Year of Inauguration

2.1 John the Baptist Prepares the Way
    8 Luke 2:40–3:6
    9 Matthew 3:4-10
    10 Luke 3:10-18
2.2 The Baptism of Jesus
    11 Matthew 3:13-17
    12 Luke 3:23a
2.3 The Temptation of Jesus
    13 Matthew 4:1-11
2.4 John the Baptist Denies Being the Messiah
2.5 Jesus the Lamb of God
2.6 Jesus' First Disciples
2.7 Jesus Calls Philip and Nathanael
2.8 Jesus Changes Water to Wine
2.9 Jesus Clears the Temple
2.10 Jesus Teaches Nicodemus
2.11 John the Baptist's Testimony About Jesus
    14 John 1:19–4:3a
2.12 Imprisonment of John the Baptist
    15 Luke 3:19-20
    16 Matthew 4:12a
    17 Luke 4:14a

2.13 Jesus Talks with a Samaritan Woman
2.14 The Disciples Rejoin Jesus
2.15 Many Samaritans Believe
2.16 Jesus Returns to Galilee
2.17 Jesus Heals an Official's Son
    18 John 4:4-54
2.18 Jesus Rejected at Nazareth
    19 Luke 4:16-30
2.19 Jesus Begins to Preach
    20 Matthew 4:13-17a
    21 Mark 1:14b-15
    22 Luke 4:14b-15

SECTION 3.
The Year of Popularity

3.1 The Calling of the First Disciples
    23 Matthew 4:18-22
    24 Luke 5:1-11
3.2 Jesus Drives Out an Evil Spirit
3.3 Jesus Heals Many
3.4 Jesus Prays in a Solitary Place
    25 Mark 1:21-38
3.5 Jesus Heals the Sick
    26 Matthew 4:23-25
3.6 A Man With Leprosy
3.7 Jesus Heals a Crippled Man
3.8 The Calling of Levi
    27 Mark 1:40-2:17
3.9 Jesus Questioned About Fasting
    28 Luke 5:33-39
3.10 The Healing at the Pool
3.11 Life Through the Son
3.12 Testimonies About Jesus
    28 John 5:1-47

3.13 Lord of the Sabbath
    30 Mark 2:23-26
    31 Matthew 12:5-7
    32 Mark 2:27-28
    33 Matthew 12:9-14
3.14 Crowds Follow Jesus
    34 Mark 3:7-12
    35 Matthew 12:17-21
    36 Luke 6:17-19
3.15 The Appointing of the Twelve Apostles
    37 Luke 6:12-13
    38 Mark 3:14b-19

The Sermon on the Mount (3.16-34)
3.16 The Beatitudes
3.17 Salt and Light
3.18 The Fulfillment of the Law
3.19 Murder
3.20 Adultery
3.21 Divorce
3.22 Oaths
3.23 An Eye for an Eye
3.24 Love for Enemies
3.25 Giving to the Poor
3.26 Prayer
3.27 Fasting
3.28 Treasures in Heaven
3.29 Do Not Worry
3.30 Condemning Others
3.31 Ask, Search, Knock
3.32 The Narrow and Wide Gates
3.33 A Tree and Its Fruit
3.34 The Wise and Foolish Builders
    39 Matthew 5:1 –8:1
3.35 The Faith of the Army Officer
    40 Matthew 8:5-13
3.36 Jesus Raises a Widow's Son
3.37 Jesus and John the Baptist
    41 Luke 7:11-35
3.38 Rest for the Tired
    42 Matthew 11:25-30

3.39 Jesus Anointed by a Sinful Woman
3.40 Jesus in Galilee
    43 Luke 7:36–8:3
3.41 Jesus and Beelzebub
3.42 The Sign of Jonah
3.43 Jesus' Mother and Brothers
    44 Matthew 12:22-50
    45 Luke 11:27-28
3.44 The Parable of the Farmer
    46 Matthew 13:1-23
3.45 A Lamp on a Stand
3.46 The Parable of the Growing Seed
    47 Mark 4:21-29
3.47 The Parable of the Weeds
3.48 The Parables of the Mustard Seed and the Yeast
    48 Matthew 13:24-34a
    49 Mark 4:33-34
3.49 The Parable of the Weeds Explained
3.50 The Parables of the Hidden Treasure and the Pearl
3.51 The Parable of the Net
    50 Matthew 13:35-53
3.52 Jesus Calms the Storm
    51 Mark 4:35-41
3.53 The Healing of a Demon-possessed Man
    52 Luke 8:26-27
3.54 A Dead Girl and a Sick Woman
    53 Mark 5:3b-43
3.55 Jesus Heals the Blind and Mute
    54 Matthew 9:27-34
3.56 Jesus Rejected Again in His Hometown
    55 Mark 6:1-5a

SECTION 4.
The Year of Opposition

4.1 The Workers Are Few
4.2 Jesus Sends Out the Twelve
    56 Matthew 9:35–10:1
    57 Matthew 10:5-42
    58 Luke 9:6a
    59 Mark 6:12b-13
    60 Matthew 11:1
4.3 John the Baptist Beheaded
    61 Mark 6:14-16
    62 Matthew 14:2d
    63 Mark 6:17-29
    64 Matthew 14:12b
4.4 Jesus Feeds the Five Thousand
    65 Mark 6:30-37a
    66 John 6:7-15a
    67 Mark 6:45
4.5 Jesus Walks on the Water
    68 Matthew 14:23-33
4.6 Jesus Heals All Who Touch Him
    69 Mark 6:53-56
4.7 Jesus the Bread of Life
4.8 Many Disciples Leave Jesus
    70 John 6:22–7:1
4.9 Clean and Unclean
    71 Mark 7:1-16
4.10 The Faith of the Canaanite Woman
    72 Matthew 15:12-28
4.11 The Healing of a Deaf and Mute Man
    73 Mark 7:31
    74 Matthew 15:30
    75 Mark 7:32-36
    76 Matthew 15:31a
    77 Mark 7:37b
4.12 Jesus Feeds the Four Thousand
4.13 The Demand for a Sign

4.14	The Yeast of the Pharisees and Sadducees	4.33	The Children of the Devil
	78 Matthew 15:31b–16:12	4.34	The Claims of Jesus About Himself
4.15	The Healing of a Blind Man at Bethsaida	4.35	Jesus Heals a Man Born Blind
	79 Mark 8:22-2 6	4.36	The Pharisees Investigate the Healing
4.16	Peter's Confession of Christ	4.37	Spiritual Blindness
4.17	Jesus Predicts His Death	4.38	The Shepherd and His Flock
	80 Matthew 16:13-26		92 John 7:2-10:21
	81 Luke 9:26	4.39	Jesus Sends Out the Seventy-two
4.18	The Transfiguration		
	82 Matthew 16:27b–17:1	4.40	The Parable of the Good Samaritan
	83 Luke 9:28c-29a		
	84 Matthew 17:2	4.41	At the Home of Martha and Mary
	85 Luke 9:30-33		
4.19	The Healing of a Boy With a Demon	4.42	Jesus' Teaching on Prayer
			93 Luke 10:1 –11:13
	86 Matthew 17:5-17	4.43	Jesus Accuses the Pharisees and the Teachers of the Law
4.20	Jesus Again Predicts His Death		
	87 Mark 9:20-32	4.44	Warnings and Encouragements
4.21	The Temple Tax		
4.22	The Greatest in the Kingdom of Heaven	4.45	The Parable of the Rich Fool
			94 Luke 11:37–12:21
	88 Matthew 17:24 – 18:5	4.46	Not Peace but Division
	89 Mark: 9:38-41		95 Luke 12:49-53
4.23	A Follower Who Sins Against You	4.47	Repent or Perish
		4.48	A Crippled Woman Healed on the Sabbath
4.24	The Parable of the Unmerciful Servant		
			96 Luke 13:1-17
	90 Matthew 18:6-35	4.49	The Unbelief of the Jews
4.25	The Cost of Following Jesus		97 John 10:22-42
	91 Luke 9:57-62	4.50	The Narrow Door
4.26	Jesus Goes to the Festival of Shelters	4.51	Jesus' Sorrow for Jerusalem
		4.52	Jesus at a Pharisee's House
4.27	Jesus Teaches at the Festival	4.53	The Parable of the Great Banquet
4.28	Is Jesus the Messiah?		
4.29	Unbelief of the Jewish Leaders	4.54	The Cost of Being a Disciple
4.30	The Woman Caught in Adultery	4.55	The Parable of the Lost Sheep
4.31	The Validity of Jesus' Testimony	4.56	The Parable of the Lost Coin
		4.57	The Parable of the Lost Son
4.32	The Children of Abraham		

4.58 The Parable of the Dishonest Manager
   98 Luke 13:22–16:15
4.59 The Rich Man and Lazarus
4.60 Sin, Faith and Duty
   99 Luke 16:19–17:10
4.61 The Death of Lazarus
4.62 Jesus Comforts the Sisters
4.63 Jesus Raises Lazarus From the Dead
4.64 The Plot to Kill Jesus
   100 John 11:1-54
4.65 Ten Men with Leprosy
4.66 The Coming of the Kingdom of God
4.67 The Parable of the Persistent Widow
4.68 The Parable of the Pharisee and the Tax Collector
   101 Luke 17:11 –18:14
4.69 Jesus' Teaching on Divorce
   102 Matthew 19:3-8
   103 Mark 10:10-12
   104 Matthew 19:10-12
4.70 The Little Children and Jesus
   105 Mark 10:13-16
4.71 The Rich Young Man
   106 Matthew 19:16-19
   107 Mark 10:20-21a
4.72 The Parable of the Workers in the Vineyard
   108 Matthew 19:21b–20:16
4.73 Jesus Again Predicts His Death
   109 Luke 18:31-34
4.74 A Mother's Request
   110 Matthew 20:20-28
4.75 Blind Bartimaeus Receives His Sight
   111 Mark 10:46-52
4.76 Zacchaeus the Tax Collector
4.77 The Parable of the Ten Servants
   112 Luke 19:1-28
4.78 Mary Anoints Jesus at Bethany
   113 John 11:55–12:2a
   114 Matthew 26:6b
   115 John 12:2b-6
   116 Mark 14:6-9

SECTION 5.
The Passion Week
5.1 The Triumphal Entry
   117 John 12:9-12
   118 Luke 19:29-36a
   119 Mark 11:8-10
   120 Luke 19:37-44
   121 Matthew 21:10-11
   122 Matthew 21:14-17
5.2 Jesus Curses the Fig Tree
5.3 Jesus Again Clears the Temple
   123 Mark 11:12-17
   124 Luke 19:47-48
5.4 Jesus Once More Predicts His Death
5.5 The Jews Continue in Their Unbelief
   125 John 12:20-50
5.6 The Fig Tree Withers
5.7 The Authority of Jesus Questioned
   126 Mark 11:19-33
5.8 The Parable of the Two Sons
5.9 The Parable of the Renters
   127 Matthew 21:28-33
   128 Mark 12:2-8
5.10 The Parable of the Wedding Banquet

5.11 Paying Taxes to the Emperor
5.12 Marriage and the Seven Brothers
5.13 The Greatest Commandment
    129 Matthew 21:40–22:36
    130 Mark 12:29-31
    131 Matthew 22:40
    132 Mark 12:32-34a
5.14 Whose Son is the Messiah?
5.15 Jesus Accuses the Pharisees and the Teachers of the Law
    133 Matthew 22:41 –23:39
5.16 The Widow's Offering
5.17 Signs of the End of the Age
    134 Mark 12:41 –13:13
    135 Matthew 24:11-31
    136 Luke 21:28-33
5.18 The Day and Hour Unknown
    137 Matthew 24:36-41
    138 Luke 21:34-36
    139 Mark 13:34-37
5.19 The Parable of the Ten Girls
5.20 The Parable of the Coins
5.21 The Sheep and the Goats
5.22 The Plot Against Jesus
    140 Matthew 24:43–26:5
5.23 Judas Agrees to Betray Jesus
    141 Luke 22:3-4
    142 Matthew 26:15-16
5.24 Preparations for the Last Supper
    143 Luke 22:7-14

The Last Supper (5.25-40)
5.25 Who is the Greatest?
    144 Luke 22:24-30
5.26 Jesus Washes His Disciples' Feet
    145 John 13:3-20
5.27 Jesus Predicts Judas' Betrayal
    146 Luke 22:15-16
    147 Matthew 26:21
    148 John 13.22
    149 Matthew 26:22
    150 John 13:23-26a
    151 Matthew 26:24-25
    152 John 13:26b-30
5.28 The Lord's Supper
    153 Luke 22:17-18
    154 Matthew 26:26
    155 Luke 22:19b-20a
    156 Matthew 26:27b
    157 Luke 22:20b
    158 Matthew 26:28b-29
5.29 A New Command
5.30 Jesus Predicts Peter's Denial
    159 John 13:31-37
    160 Matthew 26:31-33
    161 Luke 22:31-33
    162 John 13:38a
    163 Mark 14:30b-31
    164 Luke 22:35-38
5.31 Jesus Comforts His Disciples
5.32 Jesus Is the Way to the Father
5.33 Jesus Promises the Holy Spirit
5.34 The Vine and the Branches
5.35 The World Hates the Disciples
5.36 The Work of the Holy Spirit
5.37 The Disciples' Grief Will Turn to Joy
5.38 Jesus Prays for Himself
5.39 Jesus Prays for His Disciples
5.40 Jesus Prays for All Believers
    165 John 14:1 –17:26
5.41 Gethsemane
    166 Matthew 26:30
    167 Matthew 26:36-39
    168 Luke 22:43-44
    169 Matthew 26:40-46
5.42 Jesus Arrested
    170 John 18:2-9
    171 Matthew 26:48-49
    172 Luke 22:48

173 Mark 14:46a
174 John 18:10
175 Luke 22:51
176 John 18:11a
177 Matthew 26:52b
178 John 18:11b
179 Matthew 26:53-56
180 Mark 14:51-52

5.43 Jesus Taken to Annas
181 John 18:12-14
182 John 18:24
183 Matthew 26:57
184 John 18:15-16

5.44 Peter's First Denial
185 John 18:18
186 Mark 14:66
187 John 18:17
188 Mark 14:67-68

5.45 The High Priest Questions Jesus
189 John 18:19-23

5.46 Peter's Second and Third Denials
190 John 18:25a
191 Mark 14 69-70
192 John 18:26
193 Mark 14:71
194 Luke 22:60b-62

5.47 Jesus Before the Whole Council
195 Mark 14:55-56
196 Matthew 26:60b-61
197 Mark 14:58-65
198 Luke 22:66-71

5.48 Judas Hangs Himself
199 Matthew 27:1-10

5.49 Jesus Before Pilate
200 John I 8:28-38
201 Luke 23:2
202 Mark 15:4-5

5.50 Jesus Before Herod
203 Luke 23:5-12

5.51 Jesus Again Before Pilate
204 Mark 15:6-8
205 Luke 23:13-15
206 Matthew 27:17-21

5.52 Jesus Sentenced to be Crucified
207 John 19:1-15
208 Matthew 27:24-25
209 Luke 23:24-25

5.53 The Soldiers Mock Jesus
210 Matthew 27:27-31

5.54 The Crucifixion
211 Luke 23:26-32
212 Matthew 27:33-34
213 Luke 23:33-34a
214 John 19:23-24
215 John 19:19-22
216 Matthew 27:39-43
217 Luke 23:39-43
218 John 19:25-27
219 Matthew 27:45-47

5.55 The Death of Jesus
220 John 19:28-30a
221 Luke 23:46
222 Matthew 27:51-54

5.56 The Burial of Jesus
223 John 19:31-40
224 Matthew 27:60
225 Mark 15:47
226 Luke 23:56

5.57 The Guard at the Tomb
227 Matthew 27:62-66

SECTION 6.
The Last Forty Days

6. The Resurrection
    - 228 Mark 16:1a
    - 229 Matthew 28:2-4
    - 230 Mark 16:1bc-4
    - 231 Luke 24:3-5ab
    - 232 Mark 16:6ab
    - 233 Luke 24:5c
    - 234 Mark 16:6cd
    - 235 Luke 24:6b-7
    - 236 Mark 16:7
    - 237 Luke 24:8
    - 238 Matthew 28:8
    - 239 Luke 24:10-12a
    - 240 John 20:3-10
6.2 Jesus Appears to Mary Magdalene
    - 241 Mark 16:9
    - 242 John 20:11-18
    - 243 Mark 16:11
6.3 Jesus Appears to Others
6.4 The Guards' Report
    - 244 Matthew 28:9-15
6.5 On the Road to Emmaus
    - 245 Luke 24:13-35
6.6 Jesus Appears to His Disciples
    - 246 John 20:1-9a
    - 247 Luke 24:36-37
    - 248 Mark 16:14b
    - 249 Luke 24:38-43
6.7 Jesus Appears to Thomas
    - 250 John 20:20b-29
6.8 Jesus and the Miraculous Catch of Fish
6.9 Jesus Reinstates Peter
    - 251 John 21:1-23
6.10 The Great Commission
    - 252 Matthew 28:16-20a
    - 253 Mark 16:16-18
    - 254 Matthew 28:20b
6.11 Final Instructions
    - 255 Acts 1:3-4a
    - 256 Luke 24:44-49
    - 257 Acts 1:4b-8
6.12 The Ascension to Heaven
    - 258 Luke 24:50-51
    - 259 Acts 1:9b-11 I
    - 260 Mark 16:19c
    - 261 Luke 24:52
    - 262 Acts 1:12b
    - 263 Luke 24:53
6.13 The Holy Spirit Comes at Pentecost
    - 264 Acts 2:1-11
6.14 Conclusion
    - 265 Mark 16:20
    - 266 John 21:25
    - 267 John 20:30-31

Ancestry of Jesus Christ According to Matthew
- 268 Matthew 1:1-17

Ancestry of Jesus Christ According to Luke
- 269 Luke 3:23b-38

NOTES

What is the Book of Hope?

No one else has influenced the world as much as the man called Jesus. The reason for that, of course, is that Jesus Christ was not just a man. He was also God, given an earthly body so that He could save the world. The Bible explains in the New Testament the way to be saved, which is a gift from God through believing in Christ, and not by any good things that anyone can do.

Each of the men who wrote books of the Bible telling the story of Jesus (Matthew. Mark, Luke, and John] wrote with a specific purpose and audience in mind. Matthew wrote to the Jews, and so he presented Christ as the promised Messiah, their long-awaited king. Mark wrote to the Romans and presented Christ as the Servant of God. Luke wrote to the Gentiles (non-Jews) and described Christ as the Son of Man. Finally, John, who wrote to all people in general, showed that Jesus is the Son of God.

Therefore, the information we have about Jesus cannot be learned in any one of the four Gospels by itself, but only by putting the four together. Some information can be found in three of them, some in two, and some in only one of the Gospels. In The Book of Hope we have put together all the information in the order it happened. Nothing is repeated, not even when three different writers told about it. We have repeated only the teachings that Jesus gave on more than one occasion.

By putting all the events in Jesus' life together in the order they all took place, we can understand each character better. We can also see how all the places, dates, and people fit together. Reading the life of Christ in the order it probably happened helps us to know more about Jesus as a person in history. When we see the complete picture of Jesus' life, we can understand what happened during the time periods each Gospel writer chose to leave out of his story. This way we end up with a more complete account of the life of the Lord. The Bible text in this book ends with the genealogical records of Jesus Christ, one according to Matthew and the other according to Luke. These genealogies are lists of Jesus' ancestors. Matthew's list begins with Abraham [the father of the Jewish people] and follows the line of Joseph [Jesus' legal father]. Luke, on the other hand, traces the line in reverse order going back to Adam [thus showing Jesus' relationship to the whole human race] and emphasizes the line of Mary [Jesus' birth mother].